This is a story of adventure and riots and
shipwrecks and prisons and floggings and trickery and
treachery and bravery beyond belief, and love—

But it's really a story of people. Nice people,
weak people, strong people, nasty people, people
who started out weak spiritual dwarfs and ended up
strong spiritual giants, people who started out full of
doubts and ended up full of faith, people who
started out mean and nasty and ended up full of love—

It's a story of your church, and how it began,
and how it grew, until it covered the earth! But
it's also a story of men, and how they started out weak
and grew stronger and *stronger*—until they became
the UNSTOPPABLES.

You'll find your church in every page. But
more important, you'll find *yourself!*

You'll find *yourself* on every page—your
weaknesses, your strength, your problems, your snobbery,
your doubts, your faith, and yes—your TRIUMPHS!

It's the story of the UNSTOPPABLES—
one of the most thrilling stories you'll ever read!

The people who couldn't be stopped

BY ETHEL BARRETT

A Regal Venture Book
A Division of G/L Publications
Glendale, California, U.S.A.

Contents

A teaching and study guide for use with this book is available from your church supplier.

CHAPTER 1

You Have to Start *Somewhere*

Acts, chapters 1 and 2

"There's no doubt about it—I'm an absolute fizzle"

"Everything I do seems to be wrong. I can't open my mouth without putting my foot in it. And every time I think about myself, it's as if I were looking at myself in a spoon. I'm all bent out of shape."

Is that a fact? You've been walking around all this time, feeling like this? And all the time, people around you have been thinking you just had an odd disposition.

Well, move over. You're at the end of a long line.

Everybody feels like this at some time in his life, most people feel like this all too often, and some people feel like this most of the time. And anybody who has *never* felt like this, *does* have an odd disposition. He's the weird one, not you. So buck up and read on.

There was a man once, who felt like this much of the time. And he turned out to be one of the most important and dynamic men in the history of the world. When he thought about himself, it was as if he were looking at himself in Lake Galilee as he bent over his boat to pull in a fishing net, and *he* was all bent out of shape, and wavy, too.

His name was Peter, and what a rocky time *he* had of it!

Peter was a fisherman who lived near Lake Galilee. And after every fishing trip he dragged his boat up on the shore of Lake Galilee, and hauled his catch ashore, and spread his nets out to be cleaned and mended. And if his life had gone on like this he might have had an easy time of it. But one day he was tending his nets and he heard a voice. And he looked up, right into the eyes of Jesus.

"Follow me," Jesus said. And Peter's whole life went aspinning. He didn't know it at the time, but from the moment he started following Jesus, he started making history.

"But I know the score—and still I'm a fizzle"

Ah yes. You cut your teeth on Bible stories, then on Bible

2

study, and you did your homework, and it just doesn't make sense that with all this know-how, you could still be a fizzle. What's wrong, anyhow?

Well Peter knew the score, too. He knew the history of his people. He knew the history of that marvelous old city of Jerusalem, how its walls had been bashed in more than once, how it had been left in ruins, and how his people had been carried off into exile, and then had come back again and built it all up, their aching backs crying out and their hearts nearly failing them with fear and discouragement. He knew all the feast days, and all of the laws of God, and all the things the prophets of old had foretold, including a Saviour who would come bursting into history, straight from God, and set everything aright again. He knew the history of that famous and glorious Temple, and all the outer courts, and the inner courts, right up to that *very inner* and very holy place.* He knew it all, and yet somehow he didn't seem to be doing much better than you are doing right now.

"But I'm living in a goldfish bowl—and it hurts!"

What are you? A PK?† A TK?** Or an OK?‡ Are you set up as an "example" and your shoulders are sagging under the weight? Or are you an "ordinary kid" who has accepted Christ, and now you somehow have to prove that it's "for real"? Or worse yet, are you an ordinary kid who has accepted Christ, and now have to go back into a Godless home where nobody believes this wonderful new thing that has happened to you, and they're watching you like

*Called the "holy of holies."

†Preacher's kid.

**Teacher's kid.

‡Ordinary kid.

3

vultures, waiting to pounce on your every mistake? No matter which you are, it can be very, very rough.

Well Peter had the same problem. He was a *disciple*. From the moment he came face to face with Jesus and decided to follow Him, he was a disciple, and everything he did (and everything he didn't) was on display, for the vultures to pick at. And the vultures had good pickings. For poor Peter opened his mouth when he shouldn't have, and kept it closed when he shouldn't have, and all in all, did just about everything wrong in the book, all through his days with Jesus. What a wretched failure.

"But I know the Lord—doesn't that make a difference?"

It makes a difference only if you *let* it. For He is able to help you only as much as you want Him to. But even if you have only a nodding acquaintance with Him, you still have an advantage over Peter. You know that, just as the prophets foretold, Jesus was born in a manger in Bethlehem. And you know that He was the Saviour God had promised all these long years. And that He was born to die for our sins. Peter didn't know, for sure. He followed Jesus, watched Him perform miracles, heal the sick, raise the dead, in fact, do all the things the Old Testament prophets had said the coming Messiah would do.*

BUT.

Peter thought that his Jesus would set up His kingdom on earth, right then and there, and free the Jews from Roman rule. Peter was so confounded *earthy*. He couldn't see anything that wasn't right here and now.

"I have my 'highs'—but my 'lows'—yaaauk!"

Sure you have your "highs"—when you're on top of the

*Isaiah 35:5,6.

4

world and the Lord seems so real and so near. And then, out of the blue—POW. The joy is gone. The enthusiasm. And the love. And the courage. And you find that instead of being a devout Christian you're a devout coward. Miserable wretch, you.

Peter had his "highs." He reached heights none of the other disciples did. "Thou art the Christ, the Son of the living God," he said, and "Lord, let me come to you on the water!" he cried, and "Though all men deny Thee, yet will not *I* deny Thee!" he boasted. Great swelling words, these.

But he had his "lows" too. And he hit rock bottom during Passover Week.

How low can you get?

The week began high enough. The disciples went with Jesus to Jerusalem for the Passover Feast. There was that triumphant entry into the city, Jesus riding a donkey like a king, and the shouting of "Hosannah!" and the waving of palm branches. There was His teaching. And His healing. Peter was proud to be a part of it all. Then there was that unforgettable night in the Upper Room, where they went to eat their Passover Supper.* Where Jesus told them that He was going to be crucified—that He was the last sacrifice for the forgiveness of sin. And where Peter made his last boast: "Even if I must die with You, I will not deny or disown You!"†

It was right after that, that Jesus was arrested and Peter had a chance to make good his boast.

He got off to a smashing start by lopping off the ear of one of the arresting soldiers. And when Jesus was seized

---

*We still celebrate it today; it's called The Lord's Supper, or Communion.

†Matthew 26:35, "The Amplified Bible" (Grand Rapids: Zondervan Publishing House, 1965). Used by permission.

and dragged off to the high priest's house, Peter followed—from a distance—and waited outside in the courtyard. But from there on out, he came unraveled as if he had a loose string somewhere.

While he was waiting, a little serving maid came up to him. "You were also with Him," she said. "I don't know what you mean," he muttered. The unraveling began.

And another maid said to some bystanders, "This fellow was with Jesus the Nazarene."

"I do not know the man," he sputtered. He was beginning to come apart.

And later, still other bystanders said, "You certainly *are* one of them. Even your accent betrays you."

"May a curse be upon me if I'm not telling the truth—I do not even *know* the man!" he bellowed. He was undone.

Later, when he realized what he'd done, the Bible tells us he went out and wept bitterly.

"I'm lower than I've ever been before"

Yes. And God seems so far away that you're about to just give up the whole thing and decide you have to go on about your own lonely way, after all.

Well, so it was with Peter. For Jesus was put to death, and laid away in a tomb, and a great stone was rolled over the entrance, and every last hope that Peter had, went right down the drain. Jesus was *not* going to set up His kingdom on earth after all, and now nothing He'd ever said made any sense, and everything was in shambles. Peter was indeed, lower than he'd ever been before.

"But sometimes the Lord is hard to understand"

Sure He is. And you wish He were here, with skin and bones, telling you what to do, helping you to understand, showing you the way. But that is not His plan. And it was not His plan for Peter and the disciples. He had a much *greater* plan. But until they found out just what it was—what agony! What frustration!

For the next forty days, nobody, but *nobody* had a harder time trying to understand the Lord than Peter. For the most astonishing things began to happen.

First the report came that the tomb was empty, that Jesus had risen from the dead, that He was alive! That He had appeared to Mary Magdala! And then!

He began to appear to *them*—along the roadside—in the upper room where they were gathered—at the shore of Lake Galilee—*everywhere!* He just kept appearing in the most improbable places and in the most astonishing manner—and He gave them instructions—He told them they would have to continue the work He'd begun—that they must preach the gospel—that they were to be witnesses.*

Astonishing!

Then He told them that He would leave them again, to go to His Father in heaven. But that He would send *another* comforter†—the HOLY SPIRIT—to teach them, and to *help them remember* all the things He had told them before. *And to give them power.* They were to wait in Jerusalem until the Holy Spirit came.

The HOLY SPIRIT?

The Lord sure was hard to understand. They had *no* idea what He was up to. So you're no farther ahead, at this point, than they were.

"I'm still confused—"

So were they. After forty days of His appearing and disappearing, they were absolutely befuddled. What was He

---

*A witness is one who tells what he has seen and heard.
†Read John 14:15,16,26.

up to? He had been with them, He had told them—but they still did not understand.

Forty days is a long time. At any age, yours or theirs.

Forty days after His resurrection, He led them up to the Mount of Olives. It was a familiar place, they'd been there often. They were hopeful. Perhaps *now* He would tell them what it was all about. Perhaps *now* He would tell them that He had come to set up His kingdom on earth, to free them from Roman rule.

They asked Him.

"Lord, is now the time? You'll set up your kingdom and restore it to Israel—free us from Roman rule?"

Well of course it was a foolish question. But we all ask foolish questions of the Lord, now and then. Jesus was very patient.

"Only the Father sets those dates," He said, "and they are not for you to know. BUT. When the HOLY SPIRIT comes upon you—"

There it was again!

"You will receive POWER," He said, "to preach with great effect—"

What?

Power? To preach with great effect? What was THIS? Who wanted to PREACH? They just wanted Jesus to stay there and restore the kingdom!

"—to the people in Jerusalem—and to the ends of the earth," He said.

And it was final.

For before their very eyes, He began to rise in the air, and He rose and rose until He disappeared into a cloud. They stood there, straining their eyes to see the last of Him, absolutely dumbfounded.

But there was more to come. Before they could recover, two angels stood at their sides, and said, "Why are you staring at the sky? For Jesus has gone to heaven, and some-day, just as He went, He'll return."

Then the angels were gone.

The disciples looked at each other a moment.

What *now?*

And then they remembered.

WAIT IN JERUSALEM.

They didn't know what it was all about, but they decid-ed just to take Jesus at His word. And the Bible tells us that they "went back to Jerusalem with great joy."

You're confused? So were they. They had no idea what God was about, but they remembered Jesus' words, and they just did what He'd said, in simple faith. They went back to Jerusalem. And waited. And waited. And waited.

"I'm waiting, I'm waiting—"

Are you now? Well just remember that in spite of you, the universe is going along quite nicely, all in God's own good time. He's never in a hurry and He doesn't waste a minute. So don't rush it.

God waited until just the right time.

Ten more days went by. Now it was seven weeks since Jesus' resurrection.

Then Pentecost came.

The Day of Pentecost was an important one in the lives of the Jews. It was a feast day,* when they came from all over the country to celebrate the wheat harvest and give thanks to God.

The city was jammed with worshipers from many na-tions. In the Temple they were offering sacrifices and pray-ing. In the streets they were jostling, gawking, gossiping—just as they had done on this important day for years and

---

*It was also called the "Feast of Weeks," because it was seven weeks, or a "week of weeks" after the Feast of the Passover.

years. In an upper room somewhere in Jerusalem, the disciples and many other followers of Christ were gathered together to pray. It was nine o'clock in the morning.

No one had any inkling of what was going to happen.

Inside that upper room, the people who were gathered were praying—when suddenly—

A sound like the roaring of a mighty wind in the skies above them! And then it filled the house where they were staying! And then—what looked like flames or tongues of fire, filling the room, settling on their heads! And then—

They began to speak in languages they didn't even know!
THE HOLY SPIRIT HAD COME!

Outside in the streets, the jostling crowds heard the roaring in the sky above the house, and they all went arunning to see what it was all about—

And they heard the disciples speaking—but not in their own native Galilean dialect. No—they were speaking—they were speaking—

It absolutely *could* not be true, but it somehow was! They were speaking in the dialects of the people gathered outside! Yes, each person heard them speak in his own dialect!

"How can this be?" the people outside asked each other. "These men are Galileans. And here we are, from Parthis, Media, Elam, Mesopotamia, Judea, Cappadocia, Pontus, Asia, Phrygia, Pamphylia, Egypt, Libya, Rome—"

On and on. They were from just about *everywhere.*

"They're speaking in my dialect!"

"But I can understand them in *mine!*"

"They are telling of the mighty works of God!"

"Yaaa, they're drunk!"

"Yes, they've *got* to be drunk!"

Then one of the apostles* stepped forth.

*From here on out, the disciples were called apostles. An apostle is "one who is sent forth."

10

"Listen, all of you! Residents of Jerusalem and visitors alike!" he cried. "Drunk? We're not drunk! It's only nine o'clock in the morning! And it's the end of a fast—there hasn't been time to get drunk! No! What you are seeing was predicted by the prophet Joel—"

The crowd got quiet.

"Yes!" the apostle went on. "Joel predicted that, when the time came, God would pour out His Holy Spirit on believers!" And then he went on to tell them of their history— how God had promised them a Messiah—how He had come—and how they had murdered Him according to God's prearranged plan. And God had raised Him from the dead, according to His prearranged plan! God had *planned* it all, this apostle said.

And this Messiah had been Jesus Christ.

They were stunned, absolutely stunned.

*Awe*struck!

"Brothers—what should we do?" they cried.

The apostle shot back: "Each of you must turn back to God and be baptized in the name of Jesus Christ—and you shall also receive this gift of the Holy Spirit!"

Then he went on with a long sermon, telling them about Jesus and urging them to turn to Him and be saved.

And do you know what *happened?*

Three *thousand* of them believed, and accepted Jesus as the Son of God and as their Saviour, and were baptized! And the Bible tells us that "A deep sense of awe was on them all, and the apostles did many miracles."*

And these new believers met together. And worshiped together. And shared with each other.

And praised God.

But the most *amazing* part of this whole story is—the

*Acts 2:43, "The Living New Testament," Paraphrased (Wheaton: Tyndale House, Publishers, 1967). Used by permission.

apostle who stepped forth and preached so boldly that morning—was PETER!

Peter, who'd been frightened at a servant girl, Peter, who'd put his foot in his mouth every time he'd opened it, Peter, who'd been an absolute fizzle, Peter, who'd had his "highs" and "lows," Peter, who'd been so confused, Peter, who'd been waiting and doubting—

For Jesus was not around in the flesh, but He was *very much* around, nonetheless—for He'd sent back *another* person to *explain* Him and make Him *real*. That other person was the Holy Spirit. He'd come to dwell in the hearts of the believers.

Now He dwelt in Peter's heart.

And Peter was a new man!

Peter didn't know it then, but he was about to walk headlong into the beginning of the most earthshaking upheaval the world has ever known—the beginning of the church!

What's it to you?

When you accept Christ as your Saviour, that same Holy Spirit dwells in you. To comfort you. To make Jesus real to you. To give you power. And to make you a "new person."

Therefore, the Bible tells us,* *if any man be in Christ, he is a new creature: old things are passed away; behold all things are become new.*

A new you? It's not only entirely possible, but it's God's plan and desire for your life. All you have to do is ask.

*II Corinthians 5:17.

CHAPTER 2

What? Trouble Already?

Acts 3:1–4:31

"What's going on?"

"Dunno. Looks like a riot."

"It's coming from that direction."

"Over this way!"

"It's in the Temple court!"

"What's go—wait a minute. Those two chaps are in trouble."

"They're arresting them, looks like. What've they done?"

"Aren't they two of those Galileans?"

"Think so. But what've they— Ho, what's this? The *other* chap. I know him. Why he's—I can't believe it!"

. . . . . .

Nobody knew it was going to be such an earth-smashing day. Not the VIPs* in Jerusalem, going smugly about their very important business, nor the ordinary people in the streets, going about their ordinary business. And certainly not the three men who started it all.

When Jerusalem awoke that morning, it was business as usual. At dawn the sheep market came alive with bleating and heckling, as the shepherds led their flocks in through the sheepgate.

Then the narrow crooked streets came alive as the farmers and merchants poured in from the other gates, loaded down with their wares. And the little shops seemed to yawn and stretch and spill their merchandise out on the pavement—fruits and vegetables, silks, baskets, pottery, chickens . . . an endless variety of things to wear, eat, use and sacrifice.

Then the sun came, and the heat, and the washings began to blow on the rooftops and the odors of cooking

*Very important persons.

14

rose in the air. And the city teemed with people and bustled with activity.

Outside the Temple, the Court of the Gentiles was abustle, too. The squawking and bleating of sacrificial birds and animals in their cages and stalls, the cries of money changers in their booths, and tourists and sight-seers and worshipers milling about, everybody on business of his own.

By three in the afternoon, the din was still going strong when the two men wormed their way through the crowded streets and into the Court of the Gentiles. They were indeed "two of those Galileans." It was their third trip to the Temple, for they went regularly at nine, twelve and three to pray, according to the Jewish Law.

One was a young man, tall and lean and straight, his hair flowing. The other was bigger and older, his face craggy,* his eyes on fire. Both were toasted brown by the sun and the waters of Lake Galilee. They were two of our Lord's disciples—Peter and John. They headed for the Gate Beautiful, one of the main entrances to the Temple. They were two of the men who started the fracas.

. . . . . .

The third man was a beggar. He sat by the Gate Beautiful, cross-legged, his feet and ankles limp and useless. They had been that way from birth—over forty years. The sights and the sounds were familiar to him, for every day for years he'd been carried there to sit through the long weary hours and beg. People going through that gate were on the business of worshiping God, and, all things being equal, were, or should have been, feeling generous and expansive; it was a good place to beg.

*All busted up in little creases.

15

He watched the milling crowds, alert for those who headed toward the gate. When he saw the two men coming toward him, he stretched out his hands, palms up. "Alms!"* he cried.

. . . . . .

Now most people giving alms, dropped them into the outstretched hand, and hurried on, hardly glancing at the person, or indeed hardly thinking of him as a person at all.

But Peter and John stopped in their tracks.

"Alms!" the man whined again.

Peter and John regarded him intently for a moment. The Bible says, "Peter 'fixed his eyes on him.'" Then, "Look at us," said Peter. And the beggar jerked his head up expectantly, waiting for the coin to drop in his hand.

What happened next sent his head spinning.

"Silver and gold I do not have," said Peter. "But what I *do* have I give to you." And before the man could gather his senses, Peter went on, "In the name of Jesus Christ of Nazareth—WALK!" And he took the beggar by his right hand and pulled him to his feet, and—

The beggar stood for a moment in amazement, then took a step in astonishment, then began to walk, each step stronger than the last, and then he *leaped*, his feet and ankles that had been crippled all his life were as strong and sturdy as any man's.

He could—WALK!

Peter and John started into the Temple, the beggar following, leaping for joy. "Praise God!" he cried. "Praise God!" The men in the Temple, gathered for prayers, started in surprise, got up from their knees, and started toward them, astonished.

*Kind deeds, food, clothing, money, any help given to the poor. In this case the beggar meant money.

"Praise God!"

It was the beggar, now leaping about, now coming back to cling to Peter and John. They were back out of the Temple now, in the part of the outer court called Solomon's Porch. And people were running toward them from all directions.

"What's going on?"

"It's a cripple, made to walk!"

"It's the cripple who's been at the gate for years!"

"He's *always* been a cripple!"

"The one who's been crippled from birth!"

"And he's walking!"

"He's walking?"

"He's *leaping!*"

Fantastic, absolutely fantastic. Whatever was going *on?* People were crowding about now, pressing in, demanding with their shouts and with their eyes, some explanation from Peter and John.

Peter faced the crowd and raised his hand for silence. "Men of Israel!" he cried. "What is so surprising about this? And why do you look at us as though we by our own power and godliness had made this man walk?"

Well, this was a stopper. They stood in their tracks, silent.

"For it is the God of Abraham, Isaac, Jacob and of all our ancestors who has brought glory to His servant *Jesus* by doing this!"

They stirred, puzzled. The God of Abraham, Isaac, Jacob —yes. But *Jesus?*

"I refer to the Jesus whom you rejected before Pilate, despite Pilate's determination to release Him," Peter went on. "You killed the *author of life—*"

They began to murmur. This was too much.

"—but God brought Him back to LIFE again! And John

and I are witnesses of this fact, for after you killed Him—
we saw Him ALIVE!"

The murmuring exploded into shouts. By now the hubbub
could be heard clear out in the streets, and people were
running from everywhere. And by now the captain of the
Temple police and his guards were elbowing their way
through the crowd. And so were the chief priests. And so
were some of the Sadducees.*

Now you can see that this was going to lead to nothing
but trouble.

Peter went on to tell the crowd that the prophets of old
had *told* them that Jesus would come, and that all these
things would happen.

But he never finished his speech.

"God sent Jesus to *you*—to bring you blessing—!" he
cried. The Temple police were standing behind him now.

"—that you might turn away from your sins!" he shouted.
But that's all he said. They grabbed him and John and
dragged them off to prison.

The speech was over.

. . . . . .

The police scattered the crowd, and tried to get things
back to normal. But there were a lot of questions to be answered. Exactly what had happened? Two Galileans had
been arrested. For what? For doing a good deed! Then
what was the problem?

The problem was this: The Jewish Law was clear that
nobody could do a good deed in any other name but in
GOD'S name.† The religious leaders, and most of the people, did not believe that Jesus was the Son of God. The

*A Jewish religious group, very important.
†Since the time of Moses, to keep them from worshiping idols.

18

Sadducees did not believe in life after death. The chief priests did not like the idea of anyone's preaching without their special permission. And the Temple police were there to keep order.

Now here were Peter and John, healing a cripple in the name of JESUS, and declaring He is the Son of God. And saying that God raised Him from the dead and that they'd *seen Him alive*. And preaching without permission. And causing a giant-sized commotion!

Well. The problem was plain enough.

But do you know what happened? The people began to think about this problem, and they talked about what Peter had said, and they remembered what they had SEEN— and thousands of them decided to BELIEVE.

They decided to believe that Jesus Christ is indeed the Son of God. And that Peter had healed the cripple through His power.

The church of God was on its way!

But Peter and John were in prison.

. . . . . .

The next morning the Sanhedrin* met, and what a frightening bunch *they* were! Annas, the high priest, and all the lesser priests in his family, and all the scribes and elders—altogether they made a picture to shrivel the boldest prisoners, right down to a blob.

Peter and John were led in before them, along with the cripple.

"By what power, and *in whose name* did you do this thing?" they said. This was the moment for these two to stand up and be counted for Christ. And to stand up and be counted before these VIPs when they might decide to

*The HIGH Jewish court, and no mistake.

have your head, was no small matter. But Peter and John were filled with the Spirit of God. They stood straight and looked at their accusers, eyeball to eyeball.

"Rulers of the people," Peter began. They leaned forward. What would this upstart say? "If you want to know why we did a good deed to a helpless cripple and *how* it was done, then it is high time you knew—" he went on. They stiffened. "—he was healed by the name of Jesus Christ of Nazareth—the one you crucified—the one God raised from the dead. You're the *builders* of this kingdom. And you've rejected the *cornerstone!** He went on quickly, "*No* one else can save us. *No* other name under heaven has been given to man but His name. It's by *His* name we must be saved!"

What a speech! And what assurance, what boldness! From two men who were uneducated and never trained to speak in public! The members of the Sanhedrin were staggered. They recognized Peter and John as men who had been with Jesus. Had Jesus done *this* to them? And here was the lame man standing before their eyes, absolutely healed! It was enough to make you doubt your senses!

They ordered the two prisoners taken outside so they could have a private conference.

There was nothing else to do. It was humiliating.

. . . . . .

For a moment after Peter and John left, there was silence. Then they all began to talk at once.

"What are we going to *do* with them?"

"We can't deny what happened. We *know* a miracle has taken place through them."

*A stone that holds two masonry walls together at an intersection. Without it the walls would fall down.

20

"So does everybody else in Jerusalem. That's our problem."

"The only thing we can do now is try to keep it from spreading further."

"We could give them a stiff warning—tell them if they say anything more to anyone in His name—"

"It will be at the risk of their necks!"

The decision was unanimous. This was the way to go. The two prisoners were called back in.

. . . . . .

"No more speaking or teaching about Jesus—or in the name of Jesus," was the blunt order of the Sanhedrin, in a no-nonsense manner that should have settled the matter once and for all. But Peter and John were not so easy to frighten.

"And is it right in God's eyes for us to obey you rather than Him?" Peter shot back. "Judge for yourselves." And before they could muster up an answer, he went on, "We cannot *help* speaking of the things we actually saw and heard."

Good grief. What could be *done* with men like that? Punish them? They didn't dare. Why half the people in Jerusalem were praising God for what these Galileans had done in Jesus' name.

There was nothing to do but mutter more threats—and let them go. In the end, this is what the Sanhedrin did.

Humiliating!

. . . . . .

Peter and John left the Sanhedrin free men—but along with that freedom went a big "IF," and they knew it. Their necks were safe IF they did not speak about Jesus. And no more miracles, or else! This was a big enough "if" to shiver the timbers of any ordinary Christian.

The two men went back to their friends and told them all that had happened, and they all sat down to face the facts and count the cost. The facts could not be glossed over; Peter had gone "all out" for the Lord and the Sanhedrin was no court to trifle with. It was the same court that had sentenced Jesus to death; the threats were real and the cost would be grim.

What to do? Just keep quiet and lay low. Quit the whole business and go back to their fishing, or whatever. Throw up their hands on the grounds that the Sanhedrin was too powerful, that everything was against them. Ask God to somehow remove the danger and make everything nice and easy. But did they?

They did NOT.

With one accord, they all began to pray.

"Almighty Lord, who made the heaven and the earth—" Ah, that's enough to put iron in your spine, right there. When you begin a prayer like that, you've got the battle half won.

"Look at their threats—" And this is the point where they could have asked God to take the threats away. But no. They went on to say—

"And give us the courage to speak your Word with boldness, and without fear—" Bravo! "In spite of the threats!" Hooray! But they weren't finished *yet!*

"While you keep on healing and performing miracles in the name of Jesus!!!"

The prayer was ended. They had gone all out, no holds barred, they had laid their very lives on the line. Silence. And then—

The very building they were in began to shake! God answered them, and *how* He answered them! He sent the Holy Spirit down on them again with such power that the very building they were in began to shake! It was tremendous!

They got up from their knees so filled with courage and boldness and *power* that no Sanhedrin, no threats, no problems—could stop them now!

The church *was* on its way, and no mistake!

Think about it

At what points could Peter and John have "made themselves scarce" and slipped out of their difficulties? What could they have done (or *not* done)? What could they have said (or *not* said)?

What's it to you?

Ever face a Sanhedrin? All right, ever face a teacher who scoffs at God? Ever face kids who put you in a spot where you either have to speak up or shut up? Suppose you had a problem that was solved by a definite answer to prayer? And you were asked to explain. It would be easy if those who asked you were Christians. But supposing they weren't? Would you shrug it off as "circumstances"? Or would you come right out with it? What *would* you do?

And how about memorizing Hebrews 13:5b–6? It's a great verse to know!

"For God has said, 'I will never, *never* fail you nor forsake you.' That is why we can say without any doubt or fear, 'The Lord is my Helper and I am not afraid of anything that mere man can do'" (*Living New Testament*).

CHAPTER 3

"Getting Involved"
Really Costs Something

Acts 4:32–37; chapter 5

"But people won't get involved anymore"

True. Cars get stuck by the roadside and nobody stops. People get mugged and robbed and nobody helps. The poor go starving and nobody cares. Now it would make everything nice and tidy if we could say that all this indifference was going on *outside* the church. But the truth is that *some* of it is going on *inside* the church.

It was not always so.

One of the first things the people in the early church did was get involved. What? Have more than you needed when others were poor? Never. Have plenty to eat when others were hungry? Unthinkable. Have plenty to wear when others were ragged? Ridiculous! They plunged into involvement so much that the Bible says they "were all of one heart and mind." They stuck together like one big family, and those who *had*, brought their extra goods and money to the apostles, so it could be distributed to those who *didn't* have. No one claimed his belongings just for himself; they operated on a "what's mine is yours" policy.

It was great!

You have to have a motive

We have a lot of fancy talk today—jargon we call it. We have medical jargon and technical jargon—(the spacemen don't just get in or out of a spaceship; they "ingress" and "egress." And they have to be very careful with their movements so they won't harm their suits, but instead of saying "don't tear your pants," we say "don't violate the suit." Instead of saying things simply, we have a tendency to fog it up. It makes everything seem more important, somehow, if it's mysterious.

Well, in the business of behavior we have jargon, too. Instead of just saying "Why did he *do* it?" we say "What was his motivation?" And instead of saying he had a good reason, we say he was "motivated." Motivation is simply what makes you get up and *do* something.

Well now, with this in mind, why did these people in the early church do all this sharing? Why were they so eager to get involved? They were "motivated," is what they were, and no mistake. They had the greatest "motivation" for good behavior the world has ever known. They thought our Lord was coming back any minute! So when they prayed, God knew they meant it, and He filled them with His Holy Spirit. And His Holy Spirit gave them love and power such as they'd never even dreamed of before!

It is only when *you* realize that our Lord may come back at any minute (and He may—He is a lot more apt to come back at any minute *now* than He was *then*) that you will be eager to "get up and *do* something" about your Christianity. You will be properly "motivated."

How? Is there a "poor fund" in your church? Let go of some of that allowance. Share! Ask God what He wants you to do. If there's nothing going on in your church, start something! Look around you—there's plenty that you can do.

"But I'm tired of the hypocrites in the church"

Well, you cut your teeth on the word "hypocrite." A hypocrite is a person who pretends to be what he is not. A hypocrite is, in short, a "phony." Know any phonies? People who call themselves Christians, but their actions somehow don't go along with it? And so you just sit down by the roadside and decide there's no use going on? The whole thing's not for real, after all? And if you were back in the *early church,* everything would be different? Well, in Acts 5:1–11, God lets you in on a little secret; there were "phonies" in the early church, too. So simmer down, and meet the first two "phonies" on record in the early church.

Their names were Ananias and Sapphira.

They were husband and wife, and they'd joined this new group of Christians, and they were terribly excited about all this sharing that was going on. Why, a man named Barnabas had just sold his property and had given the money—*all* of it—to the apostles, to distribute among the poor.

Extraordinary!

Everyone was raving about the generosity of Barnabas. And here's where Ananias and Sapphira fell down.

They decided that they would sell a bit of property that they owned, and give it to the apostles, too. BUT. Why not be cagey? They could tell the apostles that they'd sold it for a *lesser* price, and nobody'd know the difference! They could keep back part of their money and still get all the credit and everybody would just simply rave about them, and what a good impression they'd make! They'd be every bit as popular as Barnabas, and nobody'd know the difference!

Jolly!

But it wasn't so jolly.

When they brought the money to the apostles, Peter said, "Why have you lied to the Holy Spirit? Why have you kept back the full price of the land? Before you sold it, wasn't it your own?"

It was.

"And after you sold it, wasn't the money yours, to do as you pleased?"

It was.

It was, it was, it *was*.

This was the whole point.

They could have done anything they wanted with the money, but they had *lied*—they had been "phonies"—they had pretended to be what they were not. And all to gain popularity—to "look good."

"You have not cheated men—you have cheated *God!*" thundered Peter.

27

And they were both struck down, dead. Right then and there. Before the eyes of all.

God just took them home a little early, before they got into any more mischief.

The idea of "giving your all" was purely voluntary. Nobody *had* to do it. This was the whole point. God was teaching the early church a lesson, and it was a lesson never to be forgotten. After the death of Ananias and Sapphira, a great feeling of awe settled down over the church. Clearly this Christianity was not something to "play at."

Being a "phony" was bad business.

"So why go on?"

So why go on? What nonsense. Of course there are "phonies" in the church. God told us there were, right from the start. How stubbornly *honest* the Bible is! It never pulls punches; it tells all.

There are "phonies" in school, too. And in the stores. And in the markets. And in the busses. If you stayed away from every place where phonies were, you'd never get out of bed.°

Trouble, trouble, everywhere

Sometimes it seems that way. Problems on the inside—opposition on the outside—enough to make an ordinary Christian come to a grinding halt.

The people in the early church had the same discouraging business; the mischief of Ananias and Sapphira on the inside and ominous threats from the Sanhedrin† on the

°And you might find yourself in bed with the biggest phony of all—yourself.
†The highest court of the Jews.

outside. And *they* could have come to a grinding halt. But instead—

Everything was full speed ahead.

"What? Is THIS what Christianity should be like?"

Yes—this is what Christianity should be like. Full speed ahead.

Things zoomed! They met at Solomon's Porch, and Peter (and the other apostles too) told the people over and over again the wonderful story of our Lord—that He is the Son of God—that He rose from the dead—that He is *coming again!* And people joined the new church by the thousands!

Things happened! People were healed—the sick, the lame, the blind, the deaf— Every day was miracle day! Folk brought their sick from all over Jerusalem, and from outside Jerusalem* and laid them on couches and mats—in the Temple courts and even along the streets, hoping that as Peter came by, at least his *shadow* might pass over them.

Things were exciting! What with the teaching and the learning and the sharing and the loving and the healing, this was no namby-pamby business—this was adventure!

It shook all Jerusalem!

And it shook the high priest and the Sadducees, too. They were furious. And jealous. These upstart apostles were getting too powerful for comfort. They'd been threatened. But they wouldn't frighten. They'd been warned. But they wouldn't listen. Now they had to be stopped. At once. For good.

To jail with them!

"Just when everything's going fine—POW!"

"Every time I think I'm on top of it all, along comes an-

*Yes, the good news spread over the countryside.

other problem. I could be a better Christian if it weren't for these 'pows.' "

Well, yes. When everything's going fine, naturally we want it to stay that way. Who needs problems?

The apostles were on top of it all and everything was zooming when—

Back in jail. This time all of them. This was a man-sized problem—one that threatened to stop them cold. They were thrown in jail at night, to be tried in the morning. It seemed to be all over. The high priests and the Sadducees went to bed that night, and you can be sure they were gloating. The apostles settled down in jail, and you can be sure they were praying. The long night wore on, and you can be sure something was going to happen.

It did.

"But my problem can't be solved by any human means"

Perhaps not. But God can change circumstances, change people's attitudes, drop an unexpected friend in your path —arrange all sorts of "coincidences"—in fact He can provide solutions to your problems faster than the problems can pop up—provided you are right with Him. And that you didn't create that problem yourself.*

The long night dragged on, in jail. The thing looked hopeless. And then, in the darkest hours before daybreak—

An angel of the Lord appeared in their cell! And the Bible tells us simply, that the angel let them out!†

Incredible!

"Phew! My problem's solved—now I can coast along"

You think so? Bad mistake. If you really believe that God

---

*If you did, make things right first—then watch Him work!
†What a lot the Bible leaves out! And what a story that must have been.

saved you for a purpose, that He has a job for you to do, you'll never think of coasting. On with it!

The apostles were out of jail. Did the angel tell them they could coast now, there was nothing more to do? Not on your life. The angel told them to go back to the Temple courts and *keep on telling the people about Jesus!*

It was just before daybreak.

They still had time to run for their lives. But when the dawn came, and the shopkeepers opened for business, and the people began to fill the Temple courts—there were the apostles, on Solomon's Porch—preaching!

Meanwhile, the high priest and the Sadducees summoned the Sanhedrin again. Court was called to order, the prisoners were sent for, and these VIPs waited, smacking their lips, ready to jump on the ministries of the apostles and carve them into pieces too short to hang up.

Then everything seemed to happen at once. First, the Temple police returned, breathless, to blurt out that the prisoners were gone! The prison guards were on duty, the jail doors were locked—but the prisoners were gone! Then before the astonished Sanhedrin could recover from that one, a messenger arrived, breathless, to announce that the prisoners were at that moment preaching on Solomon's Porch!

The VIPs were thrown for a loss. What a horrible development! How did it happen? And what would happen *next?* They sent the Temple police to bring the prisoners, and sat back and waited, furious.

．　．　．　．　．　．

The Temple police slunk across the court toward Solomon's Porch. They'd been sent to fetch the slippery prisoners before the court. But they had no intention of using force. Might start a riot. They might even be stoned. This

31

whole thing was weird enough; they weren't about to make it worse. Easy did it. They asked the apostles to come along quietly. And the apostles did.

"Okay, I didn't 'coast'— and things are getting worse"

Same thing happened to the apostles. But wait. The story isn't over yet.

"Did we not give you strict orders not to preach in this name?" It was the high priest addressing the prisoners. Court had begun.

"Now see what's happened!" he went on. "You have filled all Jerusalem with your teaching!"

"And what's more," he bellowed, "you are determined to lay this man's death at our door!"

Well those were the charges. Serious ones indeed. The apostles' necks were at stake.

"But sometimes I'm scared to speak up"

It isn't always easy. Scoffing schoolmates, sometimes even unbelieving parents—people who are going to give you a hard time—sometimes people who are downright frightening.

The apostles were facing the most frightening group of men it is possible to imagine. The richest, the most highly educated, the most politically important men in the country. The Sanhedrin had the kind of power our Senate has today!

Peter was the spokesman.

And he pulled no punches. He stated the most important point first. "We must obey God rather than men," he said simply. And then he laid it on the line. The Sanhedrin and the people put Jesus to death. And yes, God had raised Jesus up again—*but to be their Saviour!*

Strong words. Shocking! Before they could recover, he went on: "And we were witnesses!* We were *with* Him! Before He was crucified—and *after He rose from the dead!*"

There was silence.

Then the court was in an uproar!

The apostles were now facing a courtroom filled with men who were furious, convulsed with rage, and ready to kill them!

It sure is hard to speak up. It was harder then than it is now.

Things were never blacker!

Sometimes it seems like that. Never worse. Hopeless. It seemed like that for the apostles that morning, standing there before the Sanhedrin while, as the Bible tells us, "They took counsel† to kill them."

It was a black hour. The apostles were taken outside to wait while the arguments flew back and forth inside the court. And when the arguments were over, the apostles were called—and this was the verdict.

Death?

No! Instead, just a flogging!

The order was to flog them, but good. Thirty-nine welts they had to show for it. And then they were turned loose again!

They were warned again not to speak in the name of Jesus.

But they were free!

*A witness is one who was there, and saw and heard what was going on.
†Got into a huddle.

"Good grief, what happened? And is God still working?"

Sometimes you ask this about *your* problem. What happened? Suddenly the most unexpected things turn up, out of nowhere. Things were in shambles. And now, something, someone, has turned up and set it all straight. How on earth did it happen? And why? Is God still working for you?

Of course He is.

And He was for the apostles.

One moment they were before the angry Sanhedrin, due for certain death—and the next moment they were turned loose with just a flogging and a warning.

How did it happen? What had happened while they were outside waiting?

"The most unexpected thing— you'll never believe it!"

Sometimes it *is* hard to believe, what God will do for you. Help can come in the most unexpected ways, and from the most unexpected people, and from the most unexpected places.

Help had come to the apostles from the most unexpected source you could possibly imagine. It had come from a man right within the Sanhedrin itself!

His name was Gamaliel.

Now Gamaliel was a Doctor of Law, and a man most respected and revered by everyone in that court. Whenever he had something to say, they *listened.* And while the apostles had been outside waiting for the verdict, he'd had plenty to say.

"Be careful what you plan to do to these men," he'd said. "There have been other leaders who have risen up and got people to follow them*—but they were crushed and their

*He told about them in Acts 5:36,37; it's an interesting story.

followers were scattered. So if these men and their work are not of God, the whole thing will go to pieces. BUT."

A big but, indeed.

"BUT. If this work IS of God, you cannot stop it! Or if you try, you might find yourselves fighting against *God*."

Well this was enough to stop any court, even the Sanhedrin, in its tracks.

And it did.

This is what had happened. And *this* is why the apostles were turned loose again.

"Why not quit while I'm ahead?"

"I've done my bit, I've stood up under ridicule and some real problems. I came up all right, but now I'd like to lick my wounds for awhile and sort of lay low. Don't want any *more* trouble."

Ever feel like that?

Let's see how the apostles felt. They left the Sanhedrin, bloody from their flogging, but not discouraged at all.

AND.

They went right back to the Temple and taught. And visited homes, and taught. And *did not stop teaching and preaching Jesus Christ*. They were free, they were alive, and the orders still were: FULL SPEED AHEAD!

Like Peter had said to the Sanhedrin, "We must obey God rather than men . . ."*

---

*Acts 5:29, "Living New Testament."

CHAPTER 4

So What Else Is New?

Acts, chapters 6; 7 and 8:1,2

The city of Jerusalem was in an uproar. The mob, spilling out of the Temple courts, collided with the throngs in the streets, and in one great jumble, they all made for the East Gate, pushing, jostling, shouting, scrambling. Those in the rear, just joining the fracas, asked what was going on. Those up in front knew. A man was being dragged toward the East Gate, to be taken outside the city.

"What's going on?" cried those in the rear. The reports were jumbled. What? A man was to be stoned? A young man? Who? And why? What *happened?*

The crowd pushed on, to see.

You think problems in the church are NEWS?

This is a tale of daring-do and unbelievable courage and outrageous mischief, of sneakiness and bickering and violence and yes, even minority groups! You think anything's new in human nature? Well this tale could be in today's headlines. But it happened two thousand years ago. It happened in the early church!

It began with the bickering.

You think bickering in the church is something new?

The new church grew and grew and *grew*—by the thousands. So you can see that before long there'd be all kinds of people in it. And there were. Jews born in Palestine who spoke Hebrew. Jews from foreign countries who spoke Greek. And Gentiles,* too, from all over.

Now this was quite a hodgepodge. And they all lived together and shared their food and their money. "What's mine is yours" was the policy. Sooner or later, a "minority group"† was bound to pop up.

*They were called "Proselytes."
†Sound familiar?

37

It did. Sooner.

It was the Greek-speaking Jews. And their complaint? They weren't getting their fair share of food and money. The Hebrew-speaking Jews who were born in Palestine were being unfair to them because they were "foreigners"!

Clearly, something had to be done.

You think your church organization is something new?

The new church was having "growing pains." It had to be organized and tidied up.

For what was the apostles' first duty? To teach and preach! And how could they teach and preach if they were bogged down in distributing goods and settling bickerings? Impossible! They *had* to get organized. And the complaints jogged them into it.

The solution was simple: Choose seven men to distribute the goods and take care of the details. They must be men of good standing so that people would have confidence in them. And they must be wise. *And filled with the Spirit of God.*

This they decided to do. They chose the seven men.* And they laid hands on them (put their hands on their heads) *and prayed for them.* And sent them out to do their duties. This is how our own church organization began.†

But what does all this have to do with the mob scene in the beginning of this chapter? Plenty. For one of those seven men was the young man being dragged toward the East Gate!

---

*And some of them were Greek-speaking Jews. Smart!

†Might be fun to ask your pastor for the name of a deacon or elder in your church, take your reporter's notebook and go interview him; you'll find out how your church runs.

You think arguing in the church is new?

His name was Stephen. And he not only did his duties well, but there was something extra-special about him. He was so filled with the Holy Spirit that he could not help talking about his Lord. And he did so with such power that soon he was the talk of the church. The Bible tells us that he "perform[ed] miracles and remarkable signs among the people."* It was great! It was wonderful!

And then some of the Jews began to argue with him. They stood up in the synagogues where he was teaching, and argued and quibbled and picked and tried to make mincemeat out of his sermons. But Stephen was so filled with knowledge and power that they were no match for him. At the end of each session, they sat down in defeat. Which was not calculated to make them happy, you may be sure. Stephen had a lot of followers. But he had also collected himself some dangerous enemies.

You think sneakiness in the church is new?

Well, when they couldn't trip him up right out in the open, with everything fair and square, they switched to a new set of ground rules with no holds barred. And what they did was downright sneaky.

Now if you want to cause trouble, there's nothing like starting a sneaky little rumor, to get things going. Works every time.

Which is exactly what they did.

They hired men to spread it about that Stephen had cursed Moses and even God. Downright lie, of course. But it worked. And before you could say "Rumor is spelled

*Read Acts 6:8, "The New Testament in Modern English," copyright J. B. Phillips 1958. Used by permission of The Macmillan Company.

T-R-O-U-B-L-E," Stephen had more enemies than he could count. The result was disaster. The Jewish leaders arrested him. And dragged him off to the Sanhedrin.*

You think injustice is new?

What a tense and dramatic session *that* was! You could not match it for color and excitement in any fiction.

First, the witnesses were brought against Stephen. And this time they added to their story. Stephen was constantly speaking against the laws of Moses, they said. And speaking against their beloved Temple. And to top it all off, they said, "We have heard him say that this fellow Jesus of Nazareth will destroy the Temple, and throw out all of Moses' Law[!]"†

The witnesses were finished. Everyone in the court stared at Stephen. Would he become flustered? Hang his head? Beg for mercy?

He did none of these things.

Instead, as they stared, a remarkable thing happened. His face seemed to change. It was the same face, and yet it was mysteriously different. It was radiant. It was like the face of an angel!**

It was enough to make the bravest of them shift uncomfortably in his seat and stare at the floor. It was a tense and frightening moment.

Then the high priest broke the spell. "Are these accusations true?" he said. Everyone waited. It was Stephen's turn to speak.

And what a speech it was! He went back to the very beginning of their history, and told them of God's great love

---

*That high Jewish court, remember?
†Acts 6:14, "The Living New Testament."
**Read Acts 6:15.

for them, His great plan for them, how He had sent them prophet after prophet, and leader after leader, to show them the way. And finally how He had sent them His Son, Jesus Christ, whom they had crucified.

They ground their teeth in rage. Every face in that room was twisted out of shape with fury. But Stephen wasn't looking at the angry faces. He was looking *through* them, *beyond* them. And then he cried out the most astonishing thing!* And then—

Pandemonium!†

They put their hands over their ears and shouted, to drown out his voice. They leaped from their seats and mobbed him. "The fur flew." "The feathers flew." Any way you want to put it, it was the wildest court session the Sanhedrin had ever had.

They tore into Stephen with screams and shouts, and dragged him from the room, across the outer courts of the Temple, and into the streets. That was when the crowds began to follow, toward the East Gate.

You think "violence" is new?

Outside the East Gate, they threw him down an embankment. No doubt about it. It was going to be a stoning.

The official witnesses took off their outer robes** so they'd be free to swing those deadly stones with greater accuracy. And they laid them at the feet of a young man named Saul.‡ He watched their robes for them. He didn't actually throw any stones, but he was thinking, "Go to it. Serves him right."

*Tell you what it was in a few pages; hold your breath!

†An uproar. Not an ordinary uproar; an absolutely **wild** uproar. Good word!

**It was a Jewish law. The official witnesses had the doubtful privilege of throwing the first stones.

‡Don't forget this young man: you'll hear plenty about him later.

Then the first stone flew. Then another. And another. It was the signal for the crowd to join in, throwing rocks, pushing boulders down, and screaming in rage.

It didn't take long.

Stephen had a chance to cry out only twice. Once he said, "Lord Jesus, receive my spirit!" And then he said, "Lord, don't hold this sin against them!" And then he died.

It was all over.

The losers? The Jewish leaders. The witnesses. The people who threw the stones. And the people who *agreed* with the people who threw the stones.

The winner? Stephen.

"Hey—wait a minute—I don't get it!"

"It was all so totally unfair. How could Stephen be called a winner? And that it should happen to such a good guy! Why? And why did the whole thing have to happen in the first place?"

Good questions.

And there are some good answers.

In the first place, things were never the same again. An end had come to the time that the church could meet unafraid in Solomon's Porch or have meetings in private homes.

The deal was, now, to stamp out the new church. The believers were persecuted and threatened and hounded until, family by family, they moved out and settled all over Judea and Samaria.

The new church was *scattered.*

Why?

Because God *wanted* it to be scattered. If they'd remained right there in Jerusalem, the good news of our Lord would never have reached the "ends of the earth." It might never have reached *you.* For wherever they went, they took the gospel with them!

Get it?

The church was scattered so *you* could say: "I will sing of the mercies of the LORD forever: with my mouth will I make known thy faithfulness to all generations." (Psalm 89:1).

"I still have some questions!"

"I get it. But what about Stephen? How can *he* be called a 'winner'? He was stoned to death, wasn't he?"

Well, it all boils down to those words he cried out, back there in the Sanhedrin court.

"I see the heavens opened!" he cried. "And I see Jesus, standing, at the right hand of God!"

Stephen didn't see the angry faces. And later, he didn't see the mob coming at him. And later, he didn't see the stones coming at him. He saw JESUS—STANDING to greet him, with open arms!

Stephen knew only one thing. He had a job to do. And he did it. While he was still young. Now he might have lived to a ripe old age. And been a very good and happy man. But to him, it didn't *matter*. What mattered to him was *now*.

A job to do? *Do* it. What's ahead? Who *cares*? And he saw JESUS, STANDING TO GREET HIM.

No matter how you look at it, Stephen was a winner.

CHAPTER 5

"But I Didn't Quite Plan It This Way"

Acts, chapters 8 and 9

Things were exploding like buckshot in all directions!
What things?

Why the amazing activities of the new church! It had started out in Jerusalem and now it was setting fires all over Judea and even up in Samaria. The apostles didn't plan it that way. It never entered their minds to do anything else but stay in Jerusalem and preach Christ.

But now Stephen had been stoned, and the believers were being persecuted and moving out of town, and the old days of meeting at Solomon's Porch were gone forever.

And now the most incredible things were happening. And to the most unlikely people! Not one of them *planned* what happened to him. And not one of them *planned* to do the things he did.

Go there? Why go THERE?

There was Philip, for instance. Philip was one of the seven men chosen, along with Stephen, to distribute food and money to the needy. And when the believers were escaping from Jerusalem in droves, Philip went along, too, and settled in Samaria. Now Philip could have found himself a nice little house and looked up a few other believers for fellowship, and settled down, never to be heard of again. But instead, he began to preach. And he was so filled with the Holy Spirit, there was no stopping him. And the result?

Sensational!

Throngs of people listened to Philip preach and teach. The sick and the lame and the blind were healed, and believers were added to the church by the thousands! Philip hadn't planned it, but he went from being a quiet distributor of goods, to the man who set Samaria on fire. And just when everything was at its height, God told Philip to build a big auditorium?

No, God told Philip to leave all this excitement and success, and hike himself down south to the road that ran from Jerusalem to Gaza.*

Well Philip hadn't planned this either, but he asked no questions. He just *went*.

"Okay, I've obeyed and nothing's happening"

Philip wandered along that road without the slightest idea of what God had in store for him. Caravans went by, and merchants, and companies of soldiers, and then sometimes for long stretches—nobody at all. And then—

Along came a chariot—an elegant chariot—and in it was a dark-skinned bejeweled man, obviously someone very important. It came along slowly down the road where Philip was walking, overtook him, and clattered slowly on. And the Holy Spirit said to Philip, "Go up and walk alongside that chariot."

"What? THIS person? Why THIS person?

Sometimes the people God asks us to witness to, seem all out of joint with our plans. Why this man in the chariot wasn't even a Jew. He wasn't even a Samaritan. He was an Ethiopian.† A complete *foreigner!* Now Philip could have said all this to God, but instead he hopped to it, caught up with the chariot and walked alongside.

The Ethiopian was reading a scroll. Aloud. And Philip got the shock of his life. For the scroll was the Book of Isaiah—and the Ethiopian was reading about Isaiah's prophecy of the coming of Christ!**

"Do you understand what you're reading?" Philip asked.

*Gaza was a Philistine city, down by the Mediterranean.
†Ethiopia is in Africa.
**Isaiah 53:7,8.

"Of course not," said the man. "How can I when there is no one to instruct me?"* Whereupon he ordered his servants to halt the chariot, invited Philip to ride along with him, and the two rode on while Philip read the Scriptures and then went on to explain the birth, death, resurrection and coming-again of our Lord! And did the Ethiopian accept it? He accepted it with such enthusiasm that when they passed a small body of water, he said, "Look! Water! What is there to keep me from being baptized right now?"

"Why you *can*," said Philip, "if you believe with all your heart."

"I believe Jesus Christ is the Son of God," said the Ethiopian. "Stop the chariot!"

So Philip baptized him right on the spot. And on the way back to the chariot, the Spirit of God took Philip away suddenly, and the Ethiopian found himself alone.

But the Bible tells us, he went on his way rejoicing.

But that probably wasn't the end of it. For the Ethiopian had been to Jerusalem to worship at the Temple.† He'd come away with a scroll that told all about God. And on his way home he'd found out that this same scroll told him all about Jesus Christ too. Do you think for a moment that he was going to go home and keep *quiet* about all these wonderful things?

If he went on his way rejoicing, then he must have told everybody in sight, after he got home. And he was a man who, when *he* talked, everybody *listened*. For he was none other than the treasurer of Queen Candace of Ethiopia!

Now Philip didn't plan all this, but that chariot, rumbling down the road on its long, long journey home, was carrying the gospel with it.

*Acts 8:31, "Living New Testament."

†He'd heard about God somewhere in his travels, and went regularly to the Temple to worship with the Jews.

47

The gospel had spread to Africa!

And Philip? The Bible tells us he was next found at Azotus,* after which he made a road tour, and preached in all the cities along the coast, clear up to Caesarea.

"But these aren't the plans I had!"

Then there was Saul. He was from Tarsus,† born of devout Jewish parents, and had been sent to Jerusalem to be educated by Gamaliel,** *the* great teacher and leader of the Jewish Pharisees.

He was also the young man on page 41 who watched the robes of the men who were stoning Stephen.

And he had plans, all right, but they did NOT include spreading the new church. He had plans to *pulverize* it. After the stoning of Stephen, Saul went about like a wild bull, arresting believers, even dragging them out of their homes and hauling them off to the Sanhedrin. Then he decided to branch out, and he got a letter from the high priest, authorizing him to go up to Damascus‡ and root out believers there and drag them back to Jerusalem in chains, to be brought before the Sanhedrin. Then he started out with a company of officers from the Sanhedrin to carry out his plans. And THEN—

God stopped him in his tracks.

He and his company were almost to Damascus when it happened. Suddenly a great light from heaven spotlighted

---

*Azotus is a bit north of Gaza, right there on the Mediterranean coast.

†Tarsus was in Cicilia, a Roman province at the top end of the Mediterranean Sea. So Saul was a Jew, with Roman citizenship.

**He would have been in "Who's Who" today.

‡About 140 miles to the north, where many of the believers had fled.

upon him and blazed around him and he fell down in terror, to the dust! And he heard a voice—calling him by name!

"Saul, Saul, why are you persecuting me?"

"Who are you?" Saul said, terrified.

"I am Jesus, the one you are persecuting!" the voice came back.

And in one blinding moment, all of Saul's old beliefs went down the drain, and all his plans, and indeed all his old nature. He just lay in the dust.

"Now get up," the voice went on, "and go into Damascus, and there you'll be told what I want you to do."

The men with Saul stood there speechless. They heard the voice too, but could see no one. Saul staggered to his feet. It was then he realized that he was totally blind. They took him by the hand and led him into Damascus.

He'd planned to go in like a thunderbolt—and he went in like a frightened child. He'd planned to turn Damascus upside down—and he stumbled through its streets, led by others. Now Saul's "planning" days were over. The only plan he ever had from that time on, was God's plan for his life.

"Lord, I want your plan—but not THIS!"

Then there was Ananias. He was a believer who lived in Damascus. And like all the other believers in Damascus, he'd been hearing about the terrible persecution of the believers back in Jerusalem and especially about Saul and the mischief he'd done there. The tales came pouring into Damascus with the caravans, and with the refugees, and the tales were enough to make any believer shiver in his boots. Ananias had plans, all right. To love and serve the Lord—and to stay as far away from any persecutors as he could get.

So when the Lord came to him in a vision and said, "Ananias!"

"Yes, Lord," he said back.

"Ananias, go over to Straight Street—"

"Yes, Lord."

"—and find the house of a man named Judas—"

"Yes, Lord."

"—and inquire for a man named Saul of Tarsus—"

Who? Saul of Tarsus?

"For he is praying to me right now, and I have already given *him* a vision of *you,* placing your hands on him to restore his sight."

SAUL OF *TARSUS?*

"But Lord," sputtered Ananias, "I've heard of the terrible things that man has done to Christians in Jerusalem. And he's come here for nothing but mischief—he even has authority from the chief priests to arrest every believer in Damascus and put us all in chains!"

Madness! Go face your worst enemy and help *him? Go help a man who came here to throw you into prison?*

"I have chosen him," said the Lord, "to take the gospel to all the nations, and before kings, as well as to the Jews. So go do what I say."

Well it wasn't exactly the plan Ananias had chosen, but it was clearly *God's* plan, so Ananias carried it out.

He went over to Straight Street, found Judas' house,* asked for Saul of Tarsus, and went into the room where he was.

And there he faced his worst enemy, and there he said, "Brother Saul." *Brother* Saul! Imagine! "Brother Saul," said Ananias, as he put his hand on Saul's head, "the Lord Jesus who spoke to you on your journey here, has sent me so you may be filled with the Holy Spirit and get your sight back."

And immediately Saul could see!

*The Bible does not tell us how Saul got to Judas' house.

And the two men stood looking at each other in *love*, and to them there was only one plan that was important.

God's.

"But what if God's plan means danger?"

It sure did for Saul. His life was never the same again.

Right after he received his sight, he was baptized. And then he went off into the deserts of Arabia to be alone with this new Lord who had come upon him so unexpectedly and had changed his life and all his plans.* Then he went back to Damascus, and this time the warrants for arrest were forgotten. He began to preach the good news of Jesus, that "He is indeed the Son of God!"

"What?" cried the believers in Damascus in a mixture of fear and amazement, "Isn't this the same man who persecuted Jesus' followers so bitterly in Jerusalem?" And, "We understand that he came here to arrest them all and take them [back] in chains to the chief priest[!]"†

But Paul preached on—until they began to believe him. He became more and more powerful. He put the Damascus Jews to utter confusion with the proofs he gave them that Jesus is the Christ. And new believers cropped up everywhere! Paul's old enemies were now his friends. But his old friends (the Damascus Jews) who still would not believe, were now his enemies!

It was only a question of time before the Jewish leaders decided to finish him off.** And they posted guards by the city gates day and night, so he would not slip through their fingers.

It was also only a question of time before Paul's friends

---

*He tells about Arabia much later in his letter to the Galatians (Galatians 1:17,18).

†Read Acts 9:21, "The Living New Testament."

**Actually it was three years (Galatians 1:18).

51

heard of the plot. Damascus was a walled city, with houses built atop those walls. And one night they took him into one of those houses, and with smothered grunts and whispers, let him out one of the windows in a basket and lowered him with ropes to a little band of followers waiting down on the ground. And they started off for Jerusalem.

When they got there, the reaction was Auuuuuuuuugh! The believers there were as terrified of him as they'd been in Damascus. They thought he was faking! It was a trap!

But Barnabas* went to his rescue, took him to the apostles, explained the whole story of his change of heart, and they welcomed the old enemy, the old thunderbolt, the old terror, with open arms.

And did he preach! He preached so boldly and argued with the Jews so brilliantly that—you guessed it. Some of the Jewish leaders (with whom he had argued!) plotted to kill him.

Again he was spirited out by his friends. Spirited off to Caesarea and finally to Tarsus.

He was safe. For the time being. He knew what had happened to Stephen. He knew it could happen to him. Saul's adventures (and dangers!) had begun!†

"I didn't know the thing would reach such proportions!"

No, of course you didn't. We seldom do. For we can't see any farther than our noses, and God's plans are often farreaching beyond anything we can dream. When you deal with God, and go along with *His* plans, THINK BIG.

The church grew like wildfire, both in strength and numbers. And spread! Peter went to visit a few believers in Lydda, and there he met a man named Aeneas who'd been

*He's the chap who gave all his money, and whom Ananias and Sapphira tried to imitate.

†You'll hear more of him later.

paralyzed for eight years. "Get up and make your bed!" said Peter, and the man was instantly healed. And the *whole town* turned to the Lord when they saw Aeneas walking around!

Then Peter went to Joppa where a woman named Dorcas* was dead. And he sent the believers out, and turned to the body and said, "Get up, Dorcas!" And she did. And the news raced through the town, and *more* believers cropped up!

The gospel had spread throughout Judea and Samaria and all points east and west. And an Ethiopian had even taken it to Africa!

And the apostles had never dreamed of getting beyond Solomon's Porch!

"But I didn't plan it this way"

No. God is full of surprises. Philip didn't plan to meet an Ethiopian and get the gospel sent off to Africa, and thereby become a missionary. Ananias didn't plan to be used of God to restore the sight of the terrible Saul of Tarsus. Saul didn't plan to become a Christian and later be known as PAUL, the greatest of all apostles.

The most incredible things were happening. And to the most unlikely people! Not one of them *planned* what happened to him. It was God's great overall plan that was working.

Working to spread the gospel, to Judea, Samaria, and the uttermost parts of the earth.

And everywhere the believers went, they were sharing the Lord's Supper, witnessing, having prayer meetings, having fellowship, and sending out missionaries—the same as your church is doing today. For the church is not "buildings." The church is in the hearts of believers.

*Dorcas' story is very interesting; you can read it in Acts 9:36—43.

53

CHAPTER 6

Are You a Snob?

Acts, chapter 10; chapter 11:1–18

Ever have a sneaking suspicion that you might be a snob?*

No?

A snob is a person who thinks he's better than most people (and sometimes better than *anybody*). There are snobs who feel superior in certain areas†—musical snobs, social snobs, religious snobs—

What?

Yes. Even some of the nicest Christians can be snobs, and sometimes not even know it. They're diligent in their Bible study, enthusiastic in their youth groups and Sunday School classes, charming at their socials, and they even turn up for special prayer meetings. But they draw a little circle around themselves and their little group and post a sign (you can't *see* it, but it's there all the same): NO OUTSIDERS. No? Well, would you believe NO OUTSIDERS UNLESS THEY'RE JUST LIKE US?

"We're doing fine; let's keep it this way"

The new church was going full steam ahead. Its leaders were now scattered far and wide, preaching the good news of Jesus to Jews everywhere. Philip was in Caesarea, Saul was in Tarsus—and Peter was in Joppa. He'd stayed on, after the healing of Dorcas, and was living on the seashore at the home of Simon the tanner.**

He was preaching and teaching, and risking his life daily, willing to die for his Lord, anxious for every Jew everywhere, to hear the gospel. But in all his love and all his goodness and all his courage, it had never once entered his

---

*Being a snob is being snooty, as if you didn't already know.

†And there are snobs who feel superior in **every** area; they're **impossible.**

**A tanner of animal hides, for leather.

mind that the *Gentiles** should be included too, in the good news.

He had drawn a little circle around his own "group." NO OUTSIDERS UNLESS THEY'RE JUST LIKE US.

Peter was, alas, a snob.

Now, before you're too hard on Peter, stop and think. Peter was a Jew. The Jews were God's chosen people. They'd always been taught that they were "special"—set apart for God. Way back in the days when they were in the Promised Land, they'd been warned not to mingle with the heathen nations around them. And now, in Peter's time, they were taught not to mingle with the Gentiles.

Do business with them? Well, you could if you had to, but if you bought any cooking utensils from them you had to sterilize them with fire and water. Go into their homes? Not on your life. Invite them into yours? Never! Or if one of them *did* have to come in he was not to be left in the room alone or every bit of food or drink left on the table would be unclean. *Eat* with them? Never! Yaaaaaauk! This was Peter's training.

So Peter's little "group" was doing fine inside its little circle, and Peter wanted to keep it that way.

Now God doesn't teach us everything at once. If He did, we wouldn't be able to take it. He knows just when we need to learn each truth, and He's very, very patient. Peter had come a long way, but now he was ready for the next step. He had to be taught that God loved those *outside* Peter's circle. And that the gospel was for them too.

God taught Peter this lesson in a most amazing way, and through a man named Cornelius.

The man who was outside—WAY outside

If ever there was a man outside Peter's circle, that man

*A Gentile is anybody who is not Jewish.

was Cornelius. Cornelius was a Roman army officer,* stationed in Caesarea with Rome's occupation forces.

And the Bible tells us he was a godly man. *What?* Yes. Somewhere along the line Cornelius had forsaken the many gods the Romans worshiped, and had decided to worship the God of the Jews. The Bible tells us that he was "a godly man, deeply reverent, as was his entire household. He gave generously to charity, and was a man of prayer."†

But he was a *Roman*. Ugh. Outside. Way out. But wait.

One day Cornelius was praying—it was about three o'clock in the afternoon—when something happened that spun him around and caused him (though he did not know it at the time) to walk right into this problem of "circles," and in a most dramatic way.

An angel of the Lord appeared to him.

Now Cornelius was devout, and in the only ways he knew how, he'd been trying to get to know this God of the Jews. But never in all his born days had he ever expected to see an angel!

"Cornelius," said the angel. And Cornelius stared back at the angel in sheer terror and stammered, "What is it, Lord?"

The first part of the angel's answer was amazing—and wonderful. "Your prayers and your charities have been heard by God—and remembered." The second part of the answer was amazing—and mysterious. "Now send some men to Joppa to find a man named Peter. He's staying with Simon the tanner, by the seashore. Tell them to ask Peter to come and visit you."

Well wasn't *that* something. Peter who? And what for? Cornelius was trained as a soldier to follow orders he didn't

*He was captain of a regiment of one hundred soldiers.

†Acts 10:2, "The Living New Testament." And notice the "as was his entire household." Cornelius didn't keep his faith to himself.

57

understand. But this was the most wonderful order he'd ever received. An order from *God*.

Cornelius promptly did as he'd been told. He called two of his household servants* and a devout soldier, and sent them off on the mysterious errand.

What was going on in *Joppa?*

"I want to stay in my circle, Lord!"

The next day the sun rose bright and hot over Joppa. The little house of Simon the tanner came astir with activity. It looked like a normal day. Nobody in the house knew there were important visitors on the way. And Peter didn't know that God was going to spin him around and change all his thinking. And then, at noon, Peter was up on the roof of the house, praying, when suddenly—

He saw what seemed like a great sheet, being let down from heaven. It was suspended by its corners, and it settled to the ground. And in it were all kinds of animals and snakes and birds.† And then a voice said to him, "Get up, Peter, and kill and eat any of them you wish."

Peter was *scandalized!***

"Never, Lord," he said. "Why I've never in all my life eaten unclean creatures. They are forbidden by Jewish Law!"

"Don't contradict God," the voice came back. "If He says something is clean, it's *clean.*"

Three times, Peter saw the same vision.‡ Then the sheet was drawn back up into heaven.

---

*Cornelius sure **didn't** keep his faith to himself!

†They were kinds that Jews were forbidden to eat. See Leviticus 11:4,13,23.

**Absolutely shocked, at something that's improper.

‡God was making sure Peter learned it!

Peter sat there, thoroughly mystified. What did it mean? What on earth was he supposed to do?

Then two things happened almost at once. The voice said to Peter, "Some men are here looking for you. Don't hesitate to go with them, for I have sent them."

And downstairs, the men Cornelius had sent knocked at the gate and asked if this was the place where Peter was a guest.

It was if God were running this drama with a stopwatch!

"Okay, okay—let them in!"

Peter was not about to answer God back again. He'd already quibbled with Him over the animals in the sheet. He went downstairs at once. "I'm the man you're looking for," he said. "What brings you here?"

And they told Peter about Cornelius, what a God-fearing man he was, how an angel had appeared to him and told him to send for Peter.

And all of Peter's rules and prejudices against Gentiles went down the drain. He looked at these three Romans. And he invited them *in*. And he gave them *food*. And invited them to stay for the night!

And the next morning they started out on the long trek back—Peter and some of his believer-friends, and the three Romans. And they headed for Caesarea, and for the man who was outside the circle—way out.

"Come in—all the way in!"

It took them a day and a half to get there, but when they arrived, they found Cornelius and his family and his friends anxiously waiting to hear what God wanted them to know. And Peter went *in* the home of this Gentile, this Roman, this foreigner, without a qualm.

"You know the Jews are forbidden to associate with Gentiles or go into their houses,"* Peter told them, "but God has shown me that I should not call any man common or unclean. So I came without quibbling. Now tell me what you want."

And Cornelius told him all over again, of the wonderful experience he'd had, what the angel had said—all of it. "Now we are here," he finished, "waiting before the Lord, anxious to hear what He has told you to tell us!"†

At this moment Peter stopped being a snob. "I see very clearly," he said, "that the Jews are *not* God's only favorites! In *every* nation He has those who worship Him and do good deeds and are acceptable to Him."**

And then he began to witness to them. "I'm sure you've heard about the good news—" And he told them about God's promise of a Saviour. "And you no doubt know—" And he told them of Jesus' life on earth, and His crucifixion. "But God brought Him back to life again—" And he told them all the wonderful rest of it— The apostles had seen Him. Peter himself had seen Him. And He had told them to go out and preach the good news everywhere, before He'd been taken back up into heaven. "And," he finished, "all the prophets have written about Him, saying that [all] who believe in Him will have their sins forgiven through His name."‡

That's as far as he got.

For, even while he was speaking, the Holy Spirit fell upon them and they began speaking in different tongues, just as the believers had done on the Day of Pentecost!

*My—Peter **was** a snob!

†Acts 10:33, "The Living New Testament."

**Acts 10:34,35, "The Living New Testament."

‡Acts 10:43, "The Living New Testament." And Peter had always thought that "all" meant all the Jews; now he knew better!

Peter and the friends who'd come with him just stood there in amazement. There could be no doubt about it. The Holy Spirit had come to the Gentiles, too!

"Can anyone object to my baptizing them," Peter said finally, "now that they have received the Holy Spirit just as we did?"

No one could object.

So he did.

"You mean you went to those OUTSIDERS?"

News travels fast, and the news got back to the believers in Jerusalem before Peter did. And when he got back, did *he* ever catch it!

"You fellowshiped with Gentiles!" they bellowed.

"You went into their homes!"

"You even *ate* with them!"

Well, Peter had a lot of straightening out to do. And he told them the whole wonderful story, beginning with his vision on the roof, right up to the moment when the Holy Spirit fell upon those Gentiles the believers were so upset about. And he wound up with, "And since it was *God* who gave these Gentiles the same gift He gave us when we believed on the Lord Jesus Christ, who was *I* to argue?"*

Who indeed.

And who were *they* to argue either?

They didn't.

"You're right!" they cried. "God *has* given the privilege of turning to Jesus and receiving eternal life to the Gentiles, too!"

The little circle had broken open. God's gift of salvation was for every nation, every color, *everybody*.

Nothing would ever be the same again.

*Acts 11:17, "The Living New Testament."

"I can't be one—can I?"

Ever have a sneaking suspicion that you might be a snob? Even some of the nicest Christians can be snobs, and sometimes not even know it. NO OUTSIDERS UNLESS THEY'RE JUST LIKE US. What the Jewish believers learned through Cornelius is still true today. There can be no little circle. *Everybody* is included in God's great plan of salvation.

"For God loved the *world* so much that He gave His only Son so that anyone who believes in Him shall not perish but have eternal life."*

Be a good a idea to memorize Acts 4:12. "There is salvation in no one else [but Jesus]! Under all heaven there is no other name for men to call upon to save them."†

*John 3:16, "The Living New Testament."
†"Living New Testament."

CHAPTER 7

What? A Secret Weapon?

Acts 11:19–30; chapter 12

The circle was broken! The gospel was for everyone!

The new church began to spread like a forest fire; every time the opposition tried to stamp it out in one place, it sprang up again, and leapt to someplace else. Phoenicia—Cyprus—Antioch—

Antioch?

Why Antioch was the third largest city in the world!

It was also one of the most wicked cities in the world. The church spreading *there?*

Incredible!

But it was so.

When the word got back to the leaders of the church in Jerusalem, they stood still in amazement. But not for long. Something practical had to be done. Someone had to be sent to Antioch to investigate, and to lead. It had to be a man with a big heart, a man full of love. And a man of prayer.

Who else but Barnabas?

Why Barnabas had given his all to the church* and he had defended Saul (when all the believers had thought he was still the terrible Saul of Tarsus†). His very name meant "one who encourages."** And the Bible says he was a "kindly person, full of the Holy Spirit and strong in faith."‡

So Barnabas went off to Antioch and saw what was going on. All the reports were true. In this huge and wicked city, Jews—and Gentiles!—were being swept into the church. And because Barnabas *was* a man with a big heart, and full of love, he was not one to want to stay in his own little cir-

*Page 27.

†Page 48.

The disciples had given him this nickname. What kind of nickname do you suppose they'd give **you?

‡Acts 11:24

cle. He was *glad* it was broken, and glad God's love was for all the world.

But he had to have help. The work had grown to such huge proportions, it needed the strongest leadership Barnabas could muster. It needed a man who could talk to both Jews and Gentiles, a man who—

Wait a minute. Who else but Saul? He'd been trained by Gamaliel, the greatest of all teachers, he could reduce the arguments of the strongest Jewish leaders to mincemeat, he had Roman citizenship, *and* he was filled with the Holy Spirit and the love of God.

Barnabas went to Tarsus and looked up Saul. And in no time at all, they were both back in Antioch, working, preaching, helping, talking people right into the arms of our Lord. But they didn't draw a "circle" around Antioch, either. Part of their work was supervising the distribution of "relief boxes" to the hungry Christians in Judea.* The church was not "Antioch church" or "Jerusalem church" or "Joppa church." It was OUR LORD'S church, and it was in the hearts of the believers, *wherever* they might be.

"When you say you're a Christian you sure stick your neck out"

Yes. In school. And sometimes, if your parents aren't Christians, even at home. Takes courage, sometimes.

Did you know that it was at Antioch that the believers were first called "Christians"? And did you know it started out as a nickname to poke fun at them? "These Christ-folk," it meant, and when people said it, they said it in mockery and in contempt. "These Christ-folk," they'd sneer and "These Christ-folk," they'd hiss. But the believers just took

*They even went down to Jerusalem personally, loaded with food and gifts.

that nickname and bore it proudly, until it became a name to go down in history forever, a badge of honor.

Now some of our greatest athletes say proudly, "I'm a Christian." Even some of our Miss Americas! "I'm a Christian," they say, and nobody scoffs at them, for by their lives they've proved that they can "make it" and still carry that badge of honor with their heads up.

"Sure I believe God for this—but—"

"Sure I believe God answers prayer. But what I'm asking seems so impossible—is He really up to it?" It's hard to admit we feel like this sometimes, but we do. Or we say, "I believe I'm praying in God's will, and I'm obeying Him and I DO trust Him. My problem is great— But somehow He can find a solution."

And when He does—we're surprised!

Ever feel this way?

Well, move over. You're at the end of a long line. Christians down through the ages have underestimated God. And have been surprised when He turned out to be far greater than they'd ever dreamed possible.

There was a group of Christians in Jerusalem who prayed like this. They were gathered in the home of Mary, mother of John Mark.* Their problem was a great one—a matter of life or death.

It was about the same time Barnabas and Paul were working in Antioch. The work in Antioch was booming, but back in Jerusalem things weren't going so well. King Herod† decided things had gone smoothly just about long enough and it was time to stir up some trouble. It was the

---

*Mark later wrote the Gospel of Mark.

†And he was a "bad guy" if there ever was one.

trouble King Herod stirred up that this group of Christians was praying about.

Herod was already responsible for the execution of James.* And now he had *Peter* in prison, waiting for execution! He'd had Peter arrested during Passover Week (while the city was crowded with unbelieving Jews; good show!). As an execution was highly improper during that week, Peter had a "stay of execution," you might say. But it was only temporary. Passover was now finished. And the night this little group was praying was Peter's last night. The execution was set for morning. They prayed on. And on. Nothing happened.

"Why doesn't God TELL me what He's doing?"

Yes. If you could *see* just how God was working out your problem, it would be easier to keep believing He's going to. But often you *can't* see. Your job is to just keep on believing!

Back in prison, and unknown to those who were praying, God was working it all out.

What a prison it was! The Fortress of Antonia, high on a rock cliff northwest of the Temple, its high corner towers rising into the black Jerusalem sky. Inside was a mixture of splendor and gloom. For there were apartments and courtyards and baths. But there were also barracks for soldiers and cells for prisoners. For the Fortress of Antonia was used both as a palace and a prison.

Peter was well guarded. Outside his cell there were two soldiers. Inside his cell there were two more soldiers. And Peter was *chained to both of them*. If you were to size up Peter's situation in two words, they'd be "ungetoutable," and "insoluble."† The prison was ungetoutable and the

*Brother of John.

†This means you can't solve it—it's hopeless.

67

problem was insoluble. The only thing left for him to do was to lie there and sweat, staring into the dark gloom of the cell. But Peter wasn't sweating or staring.

He was sound asleep!

So were the guards he was chained to.

That's the way they were when the angel slapped Peter on the side and woke him up.

When Peter opened his eyes, he saw a light in the cell. Then he saw the angel. Then two things happened at once. The angel said, "Quick! Get up!" And the chains fell from Peter's wrists!

Peter thought he was dreaming; he was in a daze. "Get dressed. Put on your shoes," the angel said. Peter did. "Now put on your coat and follow me." Peter did.

It *did* seem like a dream. They went through the first and second cellblocks with no trouble or opposition. They came to the iron gate to the street—and it opened up by itself! They went out into the street and walked along about a block together—and then the angel disappeared.

Peter was alone. Out on the street. Safe. It hadn't been a dream; the whole thing was true, had actually happened. An angel had really rescued him.

He started walking through the dark deserted streets toward the house of Mark's mother, Mary.

"God answered my prayer? REALLY?"

We pray to God and then we're surprised when He answers. Sound silly? No, not really. For sometimes our problem seems so hopeless that when He untangles it and it gets solved—it *is* hard to believe! Of course we believed Him all along—but the *way* the thing got untangled— amazing!

Inside the home of Mary, the Christians were praying, when suddenly—

A knock at the outside gate!

A girl named Rhoda went out to see who it was. She unbarred the door of the house, and hurried out to the gate. "Who is it?" she said.

"It's Peter," came the voice from the other side.

Peter?

To say that Rhoda was overjoyed would be putting it mildly. She was so overjoyed that she ran back into the house with the good news—and left Peter standing there, outside the gate!

"It's Peter!" she blurted out, interrupting the prayer meeting.

"*No!*" they cried, their mouths gaping. "It can't be!"

"But it is!"

"You're out of your mind."

"No—it *really* is Peter! I heard his voice!"

"They must have killed him—it must be his ghost! What did you do?"

"Nothing! He's still out there knocking!"

Good grief!

They got stuck in doorways getting out there to see. And when they opened the gate—

It *was* Peter, in the flesh!

And these people, who'd been praying all night for Peter's safety, were surprised beyond measure when God answered their prayers!

Peter had to quiet them down before he could tell them what had happened!

He asked them to tell the others, especially James,* what had happened. And then he left for safer quarters. Their prayers had been answered, amazingly and completely.

Peter was safe.

*This James was the Lord's brother.

"Does God 'mow down' my opposition?"

God takes care of your "opposition" in many ways, and never twice the same. There are no two people alike, and no two problems alike. He may leave the opposition right there, and *you* might just become the stronger for it!

Peter's "opposition" happened to be a very wicked king who had tried to have him killed. The crime was horrible—so, so was the punishment.

If you think the surprise at the gate of Mary's house was great, imagine the surprise at the prison next morning! What had happened to Peter? And how? How could he slip through chains and guards and several gates—*how*?

Nobody knew.

When Herod sent for him, and the guards had to admit he just wasn't there, there was bedlam. The guards were tried and executed.*

And Herod?

Well, he went off in a huff to Caesarea to live for awhile. And while he was there, he made a grand speech to some delegates from other cities. It was such a grand speech that he got an ovation, along with shouts: "It is the voice of a god and not of a man!" And he accepted the people's worship, instead of giving the glory to God.

It was the last grand speech he ever made.

He was struck down by a strange illness. And before long he was dead.

So much for the opposition.

What? A secret weapon?

What made these Christians so fearless in the face of ter-

---

*Seems cruel. But it was the Roman law. A guard who let a prisoner escape, got the **prisoner's** sentence!

ror? So strong in the face of temptation? And so successful in the face of such strong opposition? You could say, "Well, God was with them" but that's too simple. He *was* with them, but there was *more* to it than that.

They had a secret.

And the secret was this. They knew the Word of God. They spent hours each day studying it. And they were great men and women of prayer.

In Bunyan's *Pilgrim's Progress*, Christian* was in the Palace Beautiful once, and the people there outfitted him with armor for warfare. They gave him the helmet of salvation, the breastplate of righteousness, the shield of faith—all of it. "Now I have everything I need to fight," he said. But they told him no. There was one thing more. And they led him to a door and opened the door and he looked inside. Nothing but a small empty room. "What's this?" he asked. And they told him it was the most important part of all his fighting equipment. It was his secret weapon. It was prayer. And all through his travels, it was part of the great secret of his strength. The other part? He carried a scroll† and he never failed to read it once each day and many times in between.

What about you?

And how about memorizing this verse: "If ye abide in me, and my words abide in you, ye shall ask what ye will, and it shall be done unto you" (John 15:7).

To abide in Him means prayer. To have His words abide in you means get that Bible off your shelf and get in it. *In* it.

*He was the hero. "Pilgrim" was his other name.

†You guessed it; it was the Word of God.

71

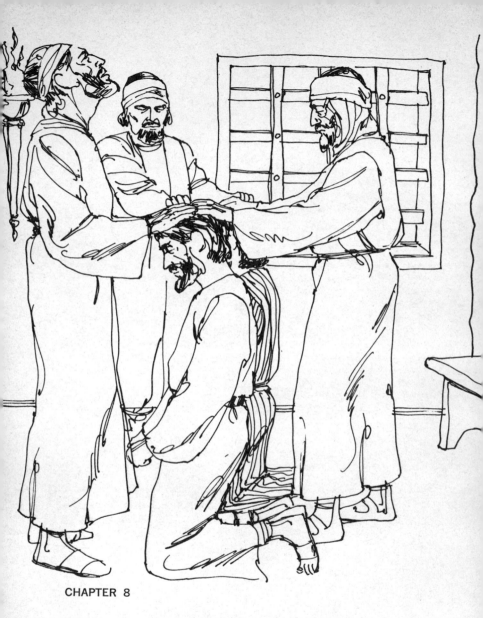

CHAPTER 8

The Anatomy of a Missionary

Acts, chapters 13 and 14

What makes a missionary tick?

Ah, yes, missionaries. Strange people. They make little farewell speeches in church, and everybody sends them off with a big hoorah, and they're gone. Then they become not people at all, but bright-colored pins *stuck* in a map, or little bulbs *screwed* in a map,* off in the church parlors somewhere. Every so often they come back with slides and show you foreign places and strange people and tell you about their work and go away again. And every so often there's a missionary drive and a missionary collection and once a year there's a "missionary conference." And *of course* you pray for them every Sunday—you just sort of stick it in—"Godblessourmissionaries"—because it's the thing to do. And before you've finished saying it, you've forgotten them entirely because they're not really people at all—just bulbs or pins. They have nothing to do with you. Or do they?

Well what makes them tick? What made them start out in the first place? Did they have a "call"? And after they *did* start out, what did they run into? People who listened to the gospel? People who didn't? What obstacles did they run into? Jealousy? Opposition? And what feelings did they have? Did they ever want to quit? Did they have terrible plunges into despair? And what temptations did they have? What? Missionaries don't have temptations?

Well they do. They have temptations and opposition and plunges and the desire to quit and all the things—all the things—

All the things that *you* do.

Because missionaries are *people*.

Just like you.

*Which is a little better, but not much.

The "call" comes first

The "call" to be a missionary isn't just a term that was invented in your church. It first happened way back in the dawn of the *early* church. And it happened this way.

Antioch was going about its business. The city was a far cry from its nickname—"Antioch the Beautiful and the Golden"—and a far cry from the quiet majestic mountains that sheltered it. It was beautiful all right, but underneath the beauty was ugliness. The people were known for their wit, their cleverness—and their wickedness.

The church in Antioch was going about *its* business. It was spreading like wildfire throughout the city, and Gentiles as well as Jews were hearing the gospel. Paul and Barnabas were back; they'd been to Jerusalem with relief bundles for the hungry Christians there, and, their job done, they'd returned and they'd brought John Mark back with them.

The church leaders were going about *their* business. It was while a group of them were praying that it happened.

Suddenly the Holy Spirit spoke to them. "Dedicate Barnabas and [Saul] for a special job I have for them."* Another way the Bible puts it is "Separate me Barnabas and Saul for the work whereunto I have called them."

So, without any quibbling, they fasted and prayed—then had a special service where they laid their hands on Saul and Barnabas† and dedicated them to God.

And the "special job"? They were to travel. They were to take the gospel abroad, farther than it had ever been before. They were to be *missionaries*.

It was the first "call" for missionaries. It happened in Antioch. And it was straight from God.

*Acts 13:2, "The Living New Testament."

†Put their hands on their heads.

"Goodbye, goodbye, God be with you"

We pack them off, our missionaries, with trunks and drums and cartons, and we pack them off with love and prayers, too, for they are very special people.

So Saul and Barnabas were packed off—with a few supplies and much love and many prayers. They left from Antioch's busy port at Seleucia, midst the screaming of parrots and the whacking of shipwright's mallets and the shouting of sailors and stevedores and the blessings of friends.

Off to the Island of Cyprus* they sailed, and headed for Salamis,† the island's largest city. There they preached and taught and brought the good news to Jews and Gentiles alike. Then from town to town, clear across the island, until they reached Paphos.

Their missionary journeys had begun.

"Oh, well. The problems have to begin sometime"

They sure do. Especially in the mission field. And "sometime" is usually pretty quick.

Paphos was a city teeming with industry** and activity. It was also teeming with idol worship.‡ And it was also teeming with superstition and magic and fortune-tellers.

Hard place to preach.

And the three missionaries' problems began right in the governor's palace.

The governor invited the missionaries to come see him, for he wanted to hear the message from God. Sounds like nothing but good news on the surface. But underneath the surface, there was trouble afoot.

---

*Cyprus was Barnabas' home territory. He was going to get a chance to witness to his old buddies!

†Salamis was full of Jews and there were probably many synagogues.

**Copper mines and shipbuilding.

‡Especially the Goddess, Venus.

In the governor's court was a man named Elymas. And Elymas was a magician, a sorcerer, a false prophet. Different translations of the Bible call him various names, all bad.

Now Elymas knew that if the governor accepted the teaching of these men, for the governor it would mean a whole new way of life. And for Elymas it would mean only one thing. The jig would be *up*. And he'd be *out*. He was jealous. And afraid. Today we'd say that his hang-up was insecurity.

Anyhow he did his best to see that he'd stay *in* and they'd be *out*. He argued with them. He tried to make their message seem like foolishness. He tried to influence the governor against them. Anything to prevent the governor from accepting this new faith!

Paul[*] knew what he was up to. And Paul put up with it just so far, and then—

He looked this rascal right in the eye, and said, "You son of the Devil, full of every sort of trickery and villainy, enemy of all that is good, will you never end your opposition to the Lord?"[†] Interesting to note that Paul did not say "opposition to *me*." No, he said, "opposition to the *Lord*."

Which was right to the point.

But Paul wasn't finished.

"Now hear this," he went on. "God Himself has laid His hand of punishment upon you."

Everyone was silent, waiting. And Elymas' mouth was shut, but good.

"And for a time—you shall be BLIND."

Instantly Elymas began to grope in the air, turning for someone to lead him. He was blind, stone-blind.

That did it.

[*]From here on out Saul was known as Paul.

[†]Acts 13:10, "The Living New Testament."

When the governor saw the power of God, he listened on to Paul's message. And he was astonished at this wonderful story of love and of our Lord. And he believed.

Elymas was *out*.

"You might want to quit"

What? Missionaries quit? Well, most of them don t, but let's face it, every once in awhile there's a dropout.

The missionaries left Cyprus and sailed to Pamphylia, a province of Asia Minor, and landed at the port of Perga. It was here that one of them decided to quit and go back home.

The "dropout" was John Mark.

We don't know why he did it—whether he was homesick or afraid of the perils ahead—but anyhow the reason couldn't have been a very good one, for Paul found it hard to forgive. The next missionary journey (much later) they took, Paul's faith in John Mark was still a bit shaky and he refused to take him along.*

"There might be a huge success"

From Perga they headed inland some 150 miles, over treacherous mountains—and over a road that was notorious for bandits. Where to? Antioch—but *another* Antioch this time. This one was in Pisidia, a Roman colony. And a *very* important city it was.

On the first Sabbath day, they went to the synagogue. When the Law had been read and the prayers had been said, the visitors were invited to speak.† " 'Brothers,' [the

*Barnabas wanted him to go; John Mark was his young cousin. And don't be too hard on Mark; he shaped up later on and wrote the Gospel of Mark.

†It was the custom then to invite visitors to speak.

synagogue officials said], 'if you have any word of instruction for us come and give it!' "*

That was all Paul needed.

" 'Men of Israel,' he said, 'and all others here who reverence God, [let me begin my remarks with a bit of history].' "†

Then Paul began his sermon.** He told them the history of the Israelites.

They listened proudly.

Then he told them about the promised Messiah.

Yes, yes, go on. They were all with him.

Then he told them of Jesus—and His sacrifice—and His resurrection—and wound up with "Everyone who trusts in Him is freed from all guilt and declared righteous—something the Jewish Law could *never* do!"‡

Well this was harder to take. But, you know—many of them *took* it! And they asked Paul to return and preach again the following week. Many of them followed the missionaries down the street as Paul urged them to accept this great salvation.

Good start!

There might be huge success— and then somebody'll come along and spoil it

The news of Paul's sermon spread like wildfire through the town via the grapevine, and the next Sabbath the synagogue was packed! Almost the entire city had turned out to hear Paul preach the Word of God.

And so *many* of them were Gentiles.

---

*Acts 13:15, "The Living New Testament."

†Acts 13:16, "The Living New Testament."

**It's the first sermon of Paul's that is recorded in the Bible.

‡Acts 13:39, "The Living New Testament." Italics added.

That was the problem.
The Jews decided to spoil it.

There may be jealousy

The Jews were jealous. They argued with Paul. They jumped on every word he said. They cursed; they tried to shout him down. Paul stood for it just so far—and then—

Paul and Barnabas threw off all their reserve and gave it to them straight. "It was necessary that the gospel be given to you first," they cried. "BUT. Since you turn it down— we'll offer it to the Gentiles!"

Some will listen!

Did the *Gentiles* ever listen! They believed, they rejoiced, they told their friends and relatives—this was God's salvation in Jesus Christ, and *they* were included! The news spread all through the city.

There may be some sneaky plots afoot

Sneaky sneaky. Know what the unbelieving Jews did? They stirred up the influential *women* to stir up their influential *husbands* to take steps against these upstarts. The women did (stir up their husbands, that is). And the husbands did (take steps to start a persecution, that is).

The result?

Rumors. Accusations. Paul and Barnabas were upstarts. The anger against them spread like wildfire.

They were finally run out of town.

You just keep on going

Did Paul and Barnabas go home, their tails between their legs, defeated and discouraged?

No, they *kept on going.* To Iconium.

Iconium was about 90 miles away. And in Iconium it was the same story all over again. Some believed. Some did not. The town was split in two. And in the end?

"STONE THEMMMMMM!!!!!!"

They fled again. But did they go home? Not on your life! They went on—to Lycaonia, Lystra, Derbe—

And the further they went the further they got from civilization. At least when they were in the cities they were under Roman law and order, and stoning was impossible. But now they were out in the boondocks.

These men were *brave.*

You could get your head turned by flattery

Flattery is pretty heady business.* Many a Christian who has stood up well under persecution has fallen on his face under flattery. Today we would say "He believed his own publicity." Bad business. It's a trap. Finish you off, every time.

Paul and Barnabas ran into it in Lystra. While Paul was preaching, all were listening. But there was one man listening whom Paul especially noticed; he had crippled feet and they'd been that way from birth. Paul saw the man's eyes, and his faith, and he looked at the crippled man and yelled, "Get up on your feet!" And the man got up on his feet—and walked!

Well the crowd went wild.

"These men are *gods!*" they shouted. "Gods in human bodies!" they yelled.

Gods? These people thought Paul and Barnabas were *GODS?*

Preposterous! *What* a development!

*Sweet talk that goes to your head; watch it!

But it was so.

The crowd actually thought that Barnabas was the Greek god Jupiter, and that Paul was Mercury!

(There was a legend that these two gods had once come down to earth in disguise. But none in all the land would accept them except two old peasants, who gave them hospitality. The result? The whole population was wiped out except for these two peasants, who were turned into two great trees when they died! And the gods had left in a huff.)

Now these people thought that the gods had come back, and they were not about to make the same mistake and ignore them again. The result?

The local priest of the temple of Jupiter brought them cartloads of flowers. And sacrificed oxen to them at the city gates. And the crowds went wild!

Now this would be enough to turn the head of anybody. (Anybody who didn't know God, that is.) Paul and Barnabas could have just settled down in Lystra and lived like kings for the rest of their lives.

But what did they do instead?

They ran out among the people and ripped their clothing in dismay. "Men!" they shouted. "What on earth are you *doing*?" And they went on to tell these poor deluded* people that they were *not* gods—but merely human beings like everybody else and that they had come to bring the gospel.

But even so, they had a hard time keeping the people from worshiping them.

You have to be prepared for the plunges

Everything's going great, and then suddenly—POW.
That's what happened.

*Misled, really mixed up. Good word. Try it sometime.

Some of the troublemakers from Antioch and Iconium had followed the missionaries to Lystra. And they picked up their dirty work where they'd left off. The result?

POW!

And a big POW it was.

Yes. These troublemakers turned the worshiping crowd into an angry mob. Paul went from being on top of the world—to being *stoned*.

Yes, *stoned*.

When they finished with him, they dragged him outside the city and left him for dead.

Talk about *plunges*!

This was a deep one.

You pick yourself up AGAIN—and go ON

Yes. Paul lay there, a crumpled heap, some believers standing around him. Then he got slowly to his feet, and stumbled forward, back into the city.

And he went *on*!

Next day Paul and Barnabas went on to Derbe. Then returned to Lystra. Back to Iconium. And Antioch. And then to Pisidia. Pamphylia. Perga. Attalia. And everywhere they went they preached the gospel. And encouraged believers to grow in the love of God and each other. And established churches. And appointed elders. And prayed for them all. And turned them over to *the care of the Lord*.

For they were living by the words of Jesus: "Therefore go and make disciples in all the nations, baptizing them into the name of the Father and of the Son and of the Holy Spirit, And then teach these new disciples to obey all the commands I have given you; and be sure of this—that I am with you always, even to the end of the world" (Matthew 28:19,20, *The Living New Testament*).

Trouble? Nonsense! They went *on*!

You come back home again—for awhile

Missionaries come back to your church, and the big map is dragged back out into the sanctuary again, with the bright-colored pins (or you light up the bulbs) and they report on their work. And they stay awhile. And then they go on their way again. But you will never know the heartbreak or the trouble they've seen. Never.

Paul and Barnabas finally sailed back to Antioch where their journey had begun, and where they had been committed to God for their great work. Which they'd completed.

They told the Christians there, how the door had been open to the Gentiles. And they stayed awhile.

And the Christians rejoiced.

But the work of the missionaries had just begun.

They'd be on their way again, soon enough.

The anatomy of a missionary

Missionaries? They make farewell speeches in your church, and then off they go, and they become pins or bulbs on a map, and then they come back again, and report. And then they go on their way again.

They have a "call." And then they run into obstacles and opposition and jealousy and temptations and terrible, terrible *plunges.*

And sometimes they want to quit.

They are *people*—just like you.

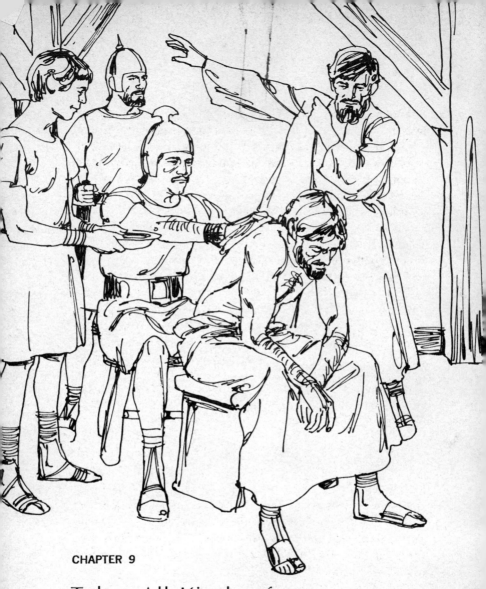

CHAPTER 9

Takes All Kinds of People to Make a Church

Acts, chapters 15 and 16

Sure does!

The "Red-and-yellow, black-and-white, we-are-precious-in-His-sight" you used to sing when you were a little kid, was talking about race and color. But "all kinds of people" means more than just that. It means rich and poor and half-way in between. It means all kinds of personalities—sweet 'n sour, bright 'n dour.* And THAT means all kinds of sur-prises—adventure, unexpected twists in the road, and, yes, problems and disputes and ticklish questions to be settled. If every Christian in the church had exactly the same per-sonality and agreed on simply everything right off the bat, how smooth-going things would be!

And how very dull.

Ugh.

The early church had a road to travel that was anything but smooth-going. Now if you want to look at this as if it were gloomsville, then you're a pessimist. But if you want to look at it as adventure and a challenge, then you're an optimist. A pessimist is a person who looks on the gloomy side: He says, "The glass is half empty. Ugh." An optimist is a person who looks on the bright side: He says, "The glass is half full. Hoooooooray!"

The "diehards"† are at it again

The church in Antioch was doing very well. Paul and Barnabas had returned from their first missionary journey, and Gentiles were being saved by just believing the won-derful news that Jesus was the Son of God, that He'd died for their sins, that He'd risen again from the dead—and that He was someday coming back!

And *then,* what happened?

*That's when you go around looking as if you'd been baptized in vinegar.

†A "diehard" is a person who stubbornly sticks to his guns even after he's been proved wrong, or after the cause is lost.

Why, some diehards from Judea went up to the Antioch church and started the whole rizzmarang all over again—the old theory that believing on Jesus was not enough—that these new Christians had to become Jews first and follow all the laws and customs of the Jews *before* they could become Christians.

Clearly, this nonsense had to be straightened out, once and for all.

Paul and Barnabas, and some local men, went back to Jerusalem* to see if they could untangle the fracas.

It's good to have leaders with clear heads

Sure is.

Paul and Barnabas met with the church members in Jerusalem. They reported on their trip, and told about the wonderful way the gospel had been opened to the Gentiles.

But it seems there were some diehards in the Jerusalem church too. They got up with long pompous† speeches and hashed the thing all over again—all the why's and wherefore's of why a Gentile had to become a Jew *before* he could become a Christian. And they really could have stalled the works, too, except for one thing.

Leaders with clear heads.

Good old Peter stood up. "Brothers," he said, "you all *know* that God told me years ago to preach to the Gentiles.** *He* made no difference between them and us. To God we are all alike! And He gave them the Holy Spirit just as He gave the Holy Spirit to us!"

*Best place to go. Jerusalem was where the church started. You might say it was the "mother church."

†Sort of lofty and high-flown. Way up-in-the-air, you know, and very, very boring.

**And he probably reminded them of Cornelius!

86

Everybody listened.

"Why should we," he went on, make it harder for the Gentiles? Make *them* keep the Law of Moses? Why, we couldn't even keep them ourselves!"

Good point.

Everybody settled down. And listened while Paul and Barnabas went on to tell them more of their adventures and how the Gentiles had been swept into the church, left and right, all along the way.

Then James stood up. Now James was the brother of our Lord, head of the Jerusalem church, and he was somebody to pay attention to! "You heard what Peter said. The Lord is bringing these people to Himself. It is my judgment—"

Everybody listened to his judgment.

It was simple. It was to the point. And it was courteous. Simply write the church at Antioch a letter saying that they* should not eat meat that had been offered to idols, and that they should keep their bodies clean and their lives pure. *That* much of the Jewish law *every* Christian should obey. But that was all. No more quibbling. The Gentiles were *welcome*.

Made sense.

Paul and Barnabas went back to Antioch. Two delegates† from the Jerusalem church went with them so it wouldn't be just a cold letter sent back, and so that everything was nice and friendly.‡

Paul and Barnabas and the two delegates went back to Antioch. The letters were read. The delegates spoke. The message was loud and clear. Gentiles, too, *could* become Christians. And the Bible tells us that there was great joy in the church.

*The Gentiles.

†Their names were Judas and Silas. And keep your eye on Silas; he turns up later on.

‡That's what was courteous. Nice going!

The fracas was over.

Phew!

It's good to have leaders with clear heads.

Now the work could go on.

"What d'you do with a 'dropout'?"

What indeed? Well you take him back, if he means business, of course. Paul and Barnabas began to embark on another missionary journey. To go back to the churches they'd established on their last journey and see how everyone was doing. Barnabas wanted to take young John Mark along again. Paul did not. After all, hadn't John Mark "dropped out" on the last one?

It was a ticklish question.

The upshot?

Well, Barnabas took Mark and sailed for Cyprus. And Paul sent to Jerusalem for Silas* and *they* set out for Cilicia. It was a ticklish question, all right. Paul and Barnabas actually split up over it.

Now.

Before we go on with the story, we have to settle poor Mark. He was a "dropout." Barnabas had faith in him. Paul did not. Mark not only "shaped up" and later wrote the Gospel of Mark, but he finally found esteem in the eyes of Paul. "Send Mark!" Paul cried in a letter from prison many years later, "for he is *profitable* to me!"

The "dropout" had sure come home. And it just might have been one of the greatest lessons in having faith in "dropouts" that Paul ever learned in his life.

Who knows?

ANYhow—

Paul and Silas went on their second missionary journey.

---

*Told you to keep your eye on him.

The church is for "half-n-half's"?

Sure. The church is for *everybody* who believes upon our Lord.

Paul and Silas went to Derbe and then on to Lystra. And in Lystra, who do you suppose they found? A young man whose mother was a Jew and had become a Christian—but his father was a Greek! His name was Timothy, and though anyone with a Jewish mother was considered a Jew, Timothy sure had a mixed-up background. And what happened to Timothy?

Paul and Silas asked him to join them! Timothy might have been a "half-n-half" but his testimony for Christ was so great that it overruled everything else!

Timothy went on with Paul and Silas, as their assistant.

The church is for all the outsiders?

Sure. *All* outsiders. Far and wide.

Paul and Silas and Timothy went on to Troas—and hit a blank spot. They did not know where to go from there. And then—

Paul had a vision.

It was a man over in Macedonia, Greece, calling out to him. And he was saying, "Come over here to Macedonia and help us!"

Well how about *that?*

Macedonia was in *Europe*. Far *far* away.

The missionaries boarded a ship at Troas and sailed straight to Samothrace and the next day to Neapolis—and then to Philippi, just inside the Macedonian border.

The church was sure for "outsiders."

The church is where you find it

Well it isn't in a building, that's for sure.

When the missionaries got to Philippi, there *were* no synagogues! So what did they do? They'd heard that a group of Christians were gathering together for a prayer meeting. So off they went to join it. And where was it?

On a riverbank!

And whom did they meet on that riverbank?

The church is for the "higher-ups"

Just one of the wealthiest women in town, that's who. Her name was Lydia.

She was a dealer in purple dye. Now purple dye had to be extracted from a certain shellfish. Drop by drop. It was hard to get. It was costly. And anybody who was a dealer in purple dye was wealthy, right up there, on top.

And what did Lydia do? She listened to the message of the missionaries, that's what. And she accepted Jesus Christ as her Saviour. And then she did the very first thing a new Christian should do; she turned her new Christianity into *good deeds*.

She invited them to stay in her home.

And they did.

The church is for the "lower-downs"

The "lower-down" was just about as low-down as you could get. She was a slave girl. Paul and Silas met her on their way down to the river for the prayer meetings. She was possessed of an evil demon, and she had the "gift" of fortune-telling, and she'd fallen into the hands of some evil men,* who used her to "tell fortunes"—and *they* collected the money.

Now this was, plainly, a "racket."

But do you know what this poor little slave girl did? She

---

*Out-and-out gangsters, is what they were.

followed Paul and Silas and kept crying out, "These men are servants of God and they have come to tell you how to have your sins forgiven!" And if you're wondering how she could say this when she was possessed with a demon, read James 2:19* where it says: "[You believe] in one God? Well, remember that the devils believe this too—so strongly that they tremble in terror!"

Anyhow, the cries of this poor girl caused such a disturbance, that Paul finally turned to her and spoke to the demon: "I command you in the name of Jesus Christ to come out of her!"

And the demon left her instantly, right on the spot, and no quibbling! In a flash, she was perfectly normal again.

And instantly her "owners" saw their income from her fortune-telling go right down the drain. And in a flash, they were FURIOUS.

The result: trouble.

Paul and Silas were snatched up without so much as a "Will you please come quietly, sirs?" and hauled off to the marketplace before the judges.

"These Jews are ruining our city!" the "owners" of the girl bellowed. "They are teaching the people to do things that are against the Roman law!"

Well, it didn't take long for a mob to form, and the judges ordered Paul and Silas stripped and beaten with wooden whips. But the horror wasn't over yet. The most vivid description of what happened next is right in Acts 16:23† "Again and again the rods slashed down across their bared backs, causing the blood to flow; and afterwards they were thrown into prison. The jailor was threatened with death if they escaped."

*"The Living New Testament."

†"The Living New Testament."

Yes. Paul and Silas were put in prison for doing *good*.

Yes, the church was for "lower-downs" too. The little slave girl had been delivered of a demon.

But it was at a terrible price.

The church is for the "in-betweens"

Yes, somewhere between the "higher-ups" and the "lower-downs" are the "in-betweens." In this case the "in-between" was the jailor at Philippi. He's better known as the "Philippian jailor" and his story is a familiar one. He was a respectable middle-class citizen, doing his duty. He didn't know God and couldn't have cared less.

He not only put Paul and Silas in prison—he put them in the *inner* dungeon of the prison and promptly clamped their feet in stocks!

The stocks were locked by a wooden bar falling into slots. And the doors of the prison were locked by wooden bars falling into slots. Everything was foolproof. The jailor ate his supper, said good-night to his family, and went to bed.* His job was done.

He had no idea that he was to meet God before the night was out.

. . . . . .

It was midnight.

The inner dungeon of the prison was damp and black, pitch black, and smelled of all the prisoners who had ever been there. The very air seemed to be filled with their cries of torment. There was nothing in that blackness but complete hopelessness and despair.

*The jailor lived somewhere on the same property.

92

The other prisoners* had settled down for another night of tortured sleep.

And then they heard something. Could it be—? Ach, no, it couldn't *possibly*. But wait a minute. It *was*. Singing? Yes, *singing!*

Those two nuts† in the inner dungeon, who'd been put there through none of their wrongdoing, and with bleeding backs, were praying and singing hymns to the Lord!

InCREDIBLE!

Why they must be out of their minds. They must be—

Wait a minute.

The ground was shaking. The *earth* was rocking. The very walls of the prison were swaying crazily, threatening to cave in! And the wooden bars were being joggled out of their slots—on the stocks—on the prison doors—and the stocks came apart—and the prison doors flew open!

Everyone in that jail was suddenly, incredibly—FREE!

EARTHQUAAAAAAAAAKE!!!

.   .   .   .   .   .

When the jailor woke up he thought it must be a nightmare. He flew out of his house. He ran toward the jail. The doors were open!

Good grief.

It was true. No nightmare, just the awful naked truth. The doors *were* open. And the prisoners had undoubtedly escaped. All of them.

And if they'd escaped, it meant only one thing. His own

*The ones in the outer prison.

†Well, **we** know they were not nuts, but the other prisoners must have thought they were.

93

death. He drew his sword to kill himself and get it all over with right then, clean and neat.

"Don't do it! Don't kill yourself! We are all here!"

It was a voice from the prison. From the *inner dungeon* of the prison.[*]

"Lights!" The jailor was trembling so he could scarcely stand.

"LIGHTS!!!"

The guards came running with torches, and he ran into the prison, through the outside corridors, into the inner dungeon.

And he saw Paul and Silas, freed from their stocks, just standing there.

And he fell down before them.

"Sirs, what must I do to be saved?" he said.

Now why didn't he say, "You still here?" or something equally as foolish? He could have said almost *anything* but "Sirs, what must I do to be saved?"

Why did he say *that*?

Because the torches weren't the only lights in that dungeon. There was a greater light dawning in his mind and in his heart. And this light had shown him his greatest need—the need to find God through our Lord.

Paul and Silas preached him the shortest sermon in the world, but it came right to the point. "Believe on the Lord Jesus and you will be saved, and your entire household," they said.

The jailor's decision was as quick as the sermon had been short. He believed. At once.

And in an instant everything had changed!

He hustled them outside, where they "told him and all

[*] It was Paul, naturally.

his household the Good News from the Lord."* Then he washed the cuts on their backs. And *then* he took them into his own home and fed them! The Bible says, "Then he brought them up into his house and set a meal before them. How he and his household rejoiced because all were now believers!"†

A night of gloom had been turned into a night of rejoicing!!

Takes all kinds of people to make a church

Yes. All races and colors. From all stations of life. With all kinds of personalities.

But there is only *one* way to God. By faith in Jesus Christ. And there is only *one* way to walk as a Christian. By that same faith. You accepted Christ and trusted Him to save you because He said He would, in His Word. Now *walk* with Him and trust Him to lead you because He said He would, in His Word. And how about memorizing this: "And now just as you trusted Christ to save you, trust Him, too, *for each day's problems;* live in vital union with Him[!]"**

P.S.:

Oh, yes. There's an interesting little postscript to the jail episode. Next morning the judges sent police officers over to tell the jailor to "let those men go!" But Paul would have none of it. "Oh, no they don't," he said. "They've beaten us in public and jailed us without trial. And we are Roman

*Acts 16:32, "The Living New Testament."

†Acts 16:34, "The Living New Testament."

**Colossians 2:6, "The Living New Testament."

citizens! Now they want us to sneak out of town. Never! Let them come in person and release us. And we'll leave town with dignity!"

Roman citizens! Horrors! When the police got back with *that* news, the judges were terrified. You just didn't *do* that to a Roman citizen, and if you did, your *neck* was at stake.

The judges did come in person, to the jailor's home, and they *begged* Paul and Silas to leave the city!

And Paul and Silas went to Lydia's house to preach one more time. And then they left town.

With dignity.

CHAPTER 10

Is This Any Way to Spread Christianity? You Bet It Is!

Acts 17

"But my problems keep reappearing"

It would be nice if each problem disappeared as soon as it was solved and never came back again. "There," we'd say, "I might have *other* problems, but I'll never have *that* one again." The fact is, though, it doesn't always work out that way. Some problems can be like pesky gnats flying in your face, coming back as fast as you brush them away.

Paul had one problem that seemed to be waiting for him around every corner. It was the little problem of riots. The story of his life begins to have a familiar ring as you read on. But in case you're thinking, "What? Another riot? When you've read one you've read them all!"—remember that each riot was terrifying and in each one Paul was risking his neck. You might say Paul's life was just one big riot-go-round. It was a problem that came around, and came around and came around . . . again . . . and again . . . and again . . .

"The problem's the same— but the CIRCUMSTANCES are different"

Yes. Sometimes the "cast of characters" is different, and the "stage setting" is different, but if you look carefully underneath, the basic problem is the same. The "plot" is the same ole plot as it always was.

After Paul and Silas left Philippi, they went to Amphipolis to Apollonia to Thessalonica. It's all told in one sentence and it takes you only seconds to read it, but from Philippi to Amphipolis was 33 miles, and from Amphipolis to Apollonia was 30 miles, and from Apollonia to Thessalonica was 37 miles, so you can see it was no afternoon stroll.

And what happened in Thessalonica?

You guessed it. A riot.

And how it started is really dirty business. The Jewish leaders were jealous and furious but they did not stir up trouble themselves.* Instead, they picked up some low-down rabble-rousing loafers—"worthless fellows from the streets," the Bible says†—and stirred them up to form a mob and start a riot. And they did a bang-up job of it, too. Different city. Different characters. Same old problem!

Sometimes you have to stick your neck out

Ever have to stand up and be counted? Ever have to really "stick your neck out" for Christianity? Would you do it if it meant embarrassment? If it meant out-and-out danger? It's something to think about!

There was a man in Thessalonica who was leading a nice safe uncomplicated life with his Christianity, until he stuck his neck out. His name was Jason. And Jason knew that Paul had an interesting history and it was spelled T-R-O-U-B-L-E. So what did Jason do? Jason took Paul and Silas and Timothy in as *houseguests*, is what Jason did.

And what did the rioting mob do? The rioting mob attacked Jason's house, is what the rioting mob did.

They couldn't find Paul and Silas there, so they settled for Jason and some believers who were in the house, and dragged them off before the council. "Paul and Silas are claiming another king named Jesus, instead of Caesar!" they bellowed. "And this Jason has let them into his home," they shrieked. "They're all guilty of treason!" they wailed. They said all this—and more.

The judges were concerned. And the VIPs** of the town were concerned. They finally let Jason and the other believers go, but only after they'd posted bail.

Jason had "stuck his neck out" for his Christianity—very far, indeed.

*The ole diehards **again!**
†Read Acts 17:5, "The Living New Testament."
**Very important person. Remember?

"The BEROEAN* Class? What's THAT?"

Do you happen to have a "Beroean Class" in your church? So many churches do! It's a favorite name for grown-up Bible classes. Funny name. Doesn't make an ounce of sense.

Well, that night (after the fracas before the council) some believers smuggled Paul and Silas out of town and "hurried"† them off to Beroea. Now Beroea was sixty miles away. So it's easy to read. But it wasn't easy to do. It was quite a jaunt.

Anyhow, the people of Beroea were open-minded and listened to Paul's preaching with eagerness. They "searched the Scriptures day by day** to check up on Paul and Silas' statements to see if they were really so."

So whenever you hear of a "Beroean Bible Class" you'll know they named it that because they meant business with God. "Beroean." Funny name. Doesn't make an ounce of sense. Until you understand what it means.

Man on the run

Paul hardly had time to unpack his duffle bag these days.

The Jews in Thessalonica learned that he was preaching in Beroea. So *they* went to Beroea. Exactly what they did there, we don't know, but the Bible tells us "they went over and stirred up trouble."‡

But before you could say "trouble in Beroea," some believers smuggled Paul off again, leaving Silas and Timothy*** behind. This time they took him to Athens. They left him

---

*Ber-ree-an.

†Acts 17:10, "The Living New Testament."

**Acts 17:11, "The Living New Testament."

‡Acts 17:13, "The Living New Testament."

***The Bible doesn't mention Timothy until verse 14, but he was right in there, pitching!

100

there, and hurried back with a message for Silas and Timothy to hurry and join him.

Paul was alone.

"I'm great if my supporters rally round"

Yes. Aren't we all?

So was Paul. But he was also great when there were *no* supporters around. In Athens he was alone. Now he could have "holed-up" in an Inn and taken a well-deserved rest until Silas and Timothy got there. But Paul was not one to either "hole-up" *or* rest. He was a man of action. And leap into action, he did. With gusto.

He went sight-seeing, to get acquainted with the city. He saw the beautiful buildings. And temples. And statues. And idols! And altars to gods! There were so many idols and altars that he could hardly turn around without bumping into one.* And yes, he even found one altar with an inscription on it: "To the Unknown God"!

He went to the synagogue too, for discussions with the Jews and some believers. And he spoke each day in the public square to anyone who'd gather round.

Now Athens was the greatest university town in the world. Just teeming with highly-educated brains. So naturally, sooner or later, Paul *had* to run into some VIP† philosophers. When he told them about Jesus and His resurrection, their reaction was, "This guy is a dreamer," and, "He's pushing some *foreign* religion."**

But they did invite him to a discussion up on Mars Hill. Whether they believed him or not didn't matter; they just *loved* to sit around and discuss new ideas. It was sort of a

*It was said of Athens "It's easier to meet a god there than a man!"

†Very important persons. Got it?

**Read Acts 17:18

city-wide pastime. Like baseball and apple pie are all-American, holding discussions was "all-Athenian." So if you were a "brain" in those days, you spent all your idle hours in "discussions" and Mars Hill was *the* place to go for this sort of business. "Come up to the discussion on Mars Hill," they invited, "and tell the other 'brains' about your ideas. For you are saying some pretty startling things."

And Paul went. With *no* supporters to rally round!

There's more than one way to witness

Paul never did have one pat little speech, when he talked about Jesus. His preaching was always made-to-order for his audience. And with this audience, he started out in the one way that would be sure to get their attention.

"I've been walking around the city, looking at all your altars to your many gods," he said, "and there was one altar with this inscription on it: 'To the Unknown God.'"

They listened. This promised to be interesting.

"You've been worshiping Him without knowing who He is," Paul went on, "and now I'd like to tell you about Him."

They were all ears.

He told them about God—about Jesus—the whole wonderful story. When he got to Jesus' resurrection, some of them laughed, but *some* of them said, "We want to hear more about this later."

But *some* of them believed!

Including a man named Dionysius, who was a member of the City Council, no less!

What are you doing with YOUR Christianity?

Remember back in Thessalonica?* And what the accus-

*Page 98.

ers bellowed to the members of the council? That Paul and Silas were traitors? Well, do you know what *else* they said? It's something you should never forget.

"These fellows," they said, and this'll bring you up with a jolt, "HAVE TURNED THE WORLD UPSIDE DOWN!!!"

It was meant as an accusation, but it was actually the greatest tribute to Paul and Silas—and to the church—that had ever been made!

What have *you* "turned upside down" with *your* Christianity? Your church? Your school? Your neighbor? *Anybody?**

Measure yourself against these men. How do you stack up?

It's quite a shocker.

*Even one person?

CHAPTER 11

A Peck of Problems—and God

Acts, chapters 18 and 19

"I'm too lofty to work"

Lots of people feel this way. "I'm too busy thinking." "I'm too intelligent." "I'm too busy trying to change the world." "I'm too busy getting it through other people's heads just what's wrong with them." "I have too many ideals. *Work?* Yaaaauk!"

Well Paul's enemies could say all sorts of things about him. But one thing they *couldn't* say. They couldn't say he was *lazy*. He was no hobo, roaming the world, trying to set it straight, too lofty to *work*. When gifts came in from his beloved church, he accepted them and spent his energies preaching the gospel. But when they didn't—he *worked*. Wherever he happened to be.

Corinth* was one of those places.

Corinth—right on the sea routes going east and west, and the land routes going north and south. Corinth—teeming with wealth, teeming with excitement—and teeming with wickedness and idol worship.

Now Paul was waiting for Silas and Timothy to join him, but Paul didn't just sit around and *wait*.† He plunged headlong into preaching the gospel. There was no money. So what did he do? He went to work, making tents, curtains, hangings, and goodness knows what else, out of a heavy cloth made of goat's hair. How did he fall into such a job? Well, first, it was a trade he'd learned as a boy. And second, he ran into a man and his wife—Aquila and Priscilla—and lo and behold if they didn't work in that very same business!

Great going!

So he lived with them and worked with them and made his living. And he preached the gospel every split second he wasn't working or sleeping!

---

*Corinth was the capital of the Roman province, Achaia.

†Paul never waited for action; he made it!

105

Brand new man. Not settled in yet. While he was new and very very green, they'd use him to help them end Paul's ministry in Corinth.

So they dragged Paul before him, and shouted "This fellow is persuading men to worship God in ways that are contrary to Roman law."

That was a half-truth, nicely twisted, and carefully calculated to turn Gallio against Paul with a vengeance. But Gallio was too smart to believe it. He saw through their little scheme at once. "There's no crime involved here," he said, "and the problem has nothing to do with Roman laws. It involves your Jewish laws and differences in your teaching. Take care of the matter yourselves!"

He refused to have anything more to do with it. And Paul was turned loose. Gallio was not indifferent.* He was simply an absolutely impartial judge.

Now back to you. If someone is trying to turn others against you, leave the matter with God.† In this case, He solved it quite nicely for Paul. If He doesn't solve it for you right away, keep your shirt on; the thing isn't over yet. Maybe the Lord is trying to teach you patience. And forgiveness.

And if someone tries to turn *you* away from someone *else* —take a lesson from Gallio. Be an absolutely impartial judge.

"The news behind the news"

We have TV programs like that today. Sometimes we call them "News in Depth." What happened *behind* the scenes? What are *all* the details? It's fun to know!

The next few laps in Paul's journey we know about, but

---

*He went down in history as a very kind man.
†Make sure you're absolutely in the right first.

only as if we were reading the headlines. No details. No "News Behind the News." He sailed for the coast of Syria and took Aquila and Priscilla with him. On to Ephesus, for a very short visit. Then back to Jerusalem for the Passover Feast.* Then back to Antioch, the very first church.

Skimpy news, what? Just headlines. What went on in the "News Behind the News"? Wouldn't you love to know? Paul never went *anywhere* without causing excitement. He was just that sort of a chap!

What, AGAIN?

Wouldn't you think he'd had enough? But no. Paul started out again on the third missionary journey.†

He trekked over all the old trail again, visiting churches and believers, and then finally, back to Ephesus. And back in Ephesus the Bible begins to give us details again—"The News Behind the News."

Miracles, miracles!

And what miracles they were! God gave Paul such power that ". . . even when his handkerchiefs or parts of his clothing were placed upon sick people, they were healed, and any demons within them came out."**

You can't really fool anybody—for long

You can't, you know. Your Christianity has *got* to be the real thing. Otherwise you're just an "Imitator." And if you are, the world will find it out soon enough.‡

---

*He left Aquila and Priscilla behind.
†He didn't have "enough" until he saw his Lord face to face.
**Acts 19:12, "The Living New Testament."
‡God knows it already.

Well, it seems there was a group of Jewish "imitators" there in Ephesus. They were magicians. They'd seen Paul's works. They'd seen him cast out demons in Jesus' name. And without really believing, without accepting Christ as their Saviour, they decided to try the same thing. Why not "imitate" Paul's Christianity? Why not use the very same name—Jesus? Why not use the chant: "I command you by Jesus, whom Paul preaches, to come out!"

Why not, indeed. The results might be interesting.

Well they tried that chant on a man possessed by a demon. And the demon cried out, right back at them: "I know *Jesus* and I know *Paul*, but who are *you?*"* And that poor demon-possessed man tore into these "imitators" with such fury that they fled out of his house half naked and badly beaten.

The results were interesting all right, but not in the way they had planned!

The story spread like wildfire throughout Ephesus. And a solemn fear of the Lord descended upon the city. Clearly this "Jesus" Paul preached was not to be taken lightly! And as the story spread, His name was spoken with awe. And with *honor.* The "imitators" were "phonies." And phonies make it for awhile—but not for long.

A "clean break" is the only way

When you're trying to "break away" from something that's wrong, you can tug a bit and then go back to it and then tug half-heartedly again and go back "just one more time." But there's just one thing wrong with this method. It doesn't work.

---

*Remember James 2:19? "Are there still some among you who hold that 'only believing' is enough? Believing in one God? Well, remember that the devils believe this too—so strongly that they tremble in terror!" ("The Living New Testament.")

The story of the demon-possessed man and the "imitators" had a deep effect on all who heard it in Ephesus. But on the *other* "imitators," it had the most astonishing effect of all. They listened to the story. They looked at themselves. And they looked at the "black magic" they'd been practicing and at their phoniness. And they dragged out all their "magic" books and charms—and dumped them in a pile—and set fire to them—and, yes, had an enormous public bonfire for all to see!

Talk about confession! Talk about meaning business! And talk about a clean break, away from sin! Why they were burning up their livelihood!

If you want to break away from something that's wrong, there's only one way to do it.

Clean break, is the only way.

The trouble with following the crowd is—

"Where's everybody going?"

"Toward the amphitheater!"

"What's going on?"

"Don't know. What're they shouting?"

"Sounds like 'Great is Diana of the Ephesians.'"

"That's what they *are* shouting. And they sound angry!"

"It's *some* sort of a blowup. Let's go!"

The crowd surged through the streets, jostling, pushing, shouting. The great amphitheater* seated 25 thousand, and in no time at all, there was standing room only.

It was a blowup, all right. A bad one.

It happened shortly after the big bonfire. And it began with a man named Demetrius.

The situation! Ephesus was the center for the worship of the goddess Diana. Her temple was there, and tourists

---

*The amphitheaters were commonly used for public meetings; they were the only places that would seat huge crowds.

poured in from all the provinces to worship—and to shop for souvenirs. And the biggest souvenir business? Little silver shrines and statues of Diana. It was a mighty poor tourist who didn't take one or the other home!

Now these Christians had invaded Ephesus, and under Paul's ministry, more believers were added daily until they were numbering in the thousands. And the tourists who were pouring in were becoming Christians too.

The problem? Hardly anyone was buying statues of Diana any more. And Demetrius was a silversmith—he manufactured them!

The solution? Well Demetrius tried to find one in the only way he knew how. The logical thing to do was to call all the silversmiths together and try to get some action, and Demetrius was a very logical man.

"Gentlemen," he began, "this business is our income. Our sales volume is going nowhere but down. And this trend is spreading throughout the entire province."

They stirred and mumbled, angry.

"Of course," he added piously, "I'm not thinking only of business. I'm thinking of the temple too. And the goddess Diana. If this keeps up, our magnificent goddess will be forgotten!"

They *boiled.* "Great is Diana of the Ephesians!" they shouted. And a crowd began to gather. "Great is Diana of the Ephesians!" they howled. And the crowd surged into the street toward the amphitheater. "GREAT IS DIANA OF THE EPHESIANS!" they shrieked. And somewhere along the way they picked up two of Paul's traveling companions and dragged them along!*

Demetrius got action all right!

.   .   .   .   .   .

*Paul wanted to go but his disciples wouldn't let him. Acts 19:30,31.

Inside the great amphitheater there was utter confusion —some shouting one thing and some another. In the midst of this bedlam, some Jews spotted a man named Alexander* and dragged him forward to speak. He raised his hands for silence, and gave it a try. But someone in the crowd shouted, "He is a Jew!" And others picked it up. "He's a Jew!!" And the crowd went wild. "HE'S A JEW!"

So they went back to their original cry. "Great is Diana of the Ephesians!" And then—

Pandemonium!†

"GREAT IS DIANA OF THE EPHESIANS!"

They kept it up for two hours!

Incredible!

Then finally someone was able to quiet them down enough to speak. It was the mayor.

"Men of Ephesus!" he cried. "*Everyone* knows that Ephesus is the home of the great Diana—her *temple* is here! So don't be disturbed. And don't do anything rash!"

The crowd listened.

"Now," he went on, "these men** you've dragged here have stolen nothing from her temple. If Demetrius and the other silversmiths have a case against these men, let them take it to our courts."

The crowd murmured, and settled down to listen again. The mayor was making sense.

"If the Roman government calls us to account for today's riot—we have no case. I wouldn't know how to explain it!"

Made sense, made sense. They listened on.

"So you are dismissed," he finished. "Now go quietly. No more hysterics."

*Alexander was apparently a leader they thought might have some influence; turned out he didn't.

†Remember that word? Look on page 41.

**Paul's traveling companions.

And they did. And there weren't. The riot was over.

But the most amazing thing about the whole fracas was: Most of the people who followed the crowd into the amphitheater and shouted themselves hoarse DIDN'T KNOW WHAT IT WAS ALL ABOUT AND DIDN'T EVEN KNOW WHY THEY WERE THERE!*

.   .   .   .   .   .

The trouble with following the crowd is—more often than not, you don't even know what it's all about, *and you don't even know why you're there.*

What about you?

If you *are* inclined to "follow the crowd," it might pay you to do some serious thinking. Just exactly what is the "crowd" up to? And just why are *you* "going along"? The answer might bring you up with a jolt.

Man with his life in his hands

Paul's friends had kept him from entering the amphitheater, and he was safe—but only for the moment. For he'd already planned to go on back through Greece and then to his beloved Jerusalem.† And there was danger ahead, every step of the way. Paul was ever ready to risk his neck for the gospel. And he was going to risk it. Again. And again. And again . . .

---

*Acts 19:32, "The Living New Testament."
†His two assistants, Timothy and Erastus, had gone on ahead.

CHAPTER 12

On with It—the Goal's in Sight!

Acts, chapters 20–23

Does your Christianity sometimes get uncomfortable?

You know, those little slights at school—sometimes downright opposition. And those little inconveniences—spending time on projects when sometimes you'd rather be spending time on yourself, even if it's just staring into space. Or daydreaming.

Well Paul's Christianity sometimes got mighty uncomfortable and inconvenient. But he seemed to delight in it. And we don't have a clue in the Bible that he ever wavered, even when it got downright dangerous.

When he left Ephesus, his travel schedule was enough to kill a man twice his size and three times as strong. His goal was Jerusalem—but oh, the stops along the way! First through Greece, preaching to believers all along the way. Then he planned to sail to Syria, but he got wind of a plot (by some Jews) against his life. They probably planned to just pop him overboard on the way. Anyhow he went by land to Macedonia instead. Then on to Philippi, stopping in cities and preaching along the way. And finally to Troas. But this brief rundown on Paul's travel schedule covers more than a year of discomfort, danger—and adventure! The exciting stories behind these few verses* would probably fill a book!

Does time in our Lord's house sometimes seem too long?

Do you sometimes get "itchy" in Sunday School? Or in the church service? Or listening to a conference speaker? Does the hour ever seem to drag? We'll grant that *some* speakers are so dull they'd make even *Paul* fidget, were he in the audience—but that doesn't happen very often. So it isn't quite cricket to blame it on the speaker. Could it be *you*, with your mind on a thousand other things? And is an hour too much to spend with the Word of God?

*Acts 20:1–6.

When the early Christians met, they really meant business. The services went on for hours sometimes. Everything was so new and exciting and there was so much to talk about! When the services were held in the evening, they went on until all hours. There was a service in Troas that went on like that. It was Paul's last night there. And he had so much to tell them and there was so much they were eager to hear, nobody wanted to break it up!

They were meeting in a large upstairs room, and the believers were stuffed in so tightly they were sitting* in every available space, including on the windowsills. The oil lamps were flickering.† Though the window shutters were open, the room was stuffy. A young chap by the name of Eutychus was sitting on a windowsill. And his head began to nod.

Paul preached on.

The oil lamps flickered away. The room got stuffier. Eutychus began to sag.

Paul preached on.

The room got *stuffier*. Eutychus fell sound asleep.

Paul preached on. And suddenly—

There was a swish of garments and a sound of toppling —and then—

A dull THUD in the courtyard, three stories below!

Everyone looked toward the window.

Eutychus was gone!

Horrors!

They scrambled to their feet and got stuck in the doorway trying to get out. He'd surely be dead. They got stuck on the stairways getting down to the courtyard. He'd *surely* be dead.

He was.

*And standing too, probably!
†And using up the oxygen!

Paul was there first. He gathered Eutychus in his arms. And he looked up into their frightened faces. "Don't be alarmed," he said. "He is not dead now. He is all right."

And he was!

Well they all went back upstairs. And observed the Lord's Supper. And Paul talked earnestly with them—until dawn!

It may not have been the *longest* service on record—but it surely was one of the most exciting!

One thing is sure—*Eutychus* never forgot it!

You think "Christian leaders" are made of stone?

The killing travel schedule went on. Paul's traveling companions went to Assos* by ship. Paul, who perhaps just wanted to be alone, went by land. They met there and sailed together to Mitylene. Then on, past Chios, Samos, and finally to Miletus. Paul had decided not to stop at Ephesus for he was in a hurry to get to Jerusalem for the celebration of Pentecost. But he sent a message for the leaders of the Ephesus church to come down to the boat to meet him.

And what a meeting it was!

"You know I have done the Lord's work humbly," Paul said, "and that I have never shrunk from telling you the truth. The necessity of turning to God through faith in our Lord."

Yes, they knew.

"And now I must go to Jerusalem," he went on. "I don't know what's ahead. But the Holy Spirit has told me that it will be jail and suffering."

They stared back at him in grief. And then he said something worth remembering:

*About 30 miles away.

118

"But life is worth nothing unless I use it for the work assigned me by the Lord Jesus—the work of telling others the Good News about God's mighty kindness and love."

They nodded, agreeing.

"You will never see my face again," he said simply.

They looked back at him. They knew, they *knew*.

And then he knelt and prayed with them. And they embraced him and said good-bye. And wept.

And then they went down to the ship to see him off.

And they wept again as he left.

They knew he would never be back. And he knew it too.

Christian "Leaders" have hearts of stone? Don't you believe it!

On with it!

Yes, on with it.

And Paul sure went "on with it." On to Cos, on to Rhodes, on to Patara, on to Tyre, on to Ptolemais, on to Caesarea—

And all along the way, believers warned him not to go to Jerusalem. In Caesarea, a man named Agabus, who had the gift of prophecy, warned him that he'd be bound in Jerusalem and turned over to the Romans. And the people *begged* him not to go. And Paul's answer is something to tack up on your mirror and look at every morning. "Why all this weeping?" he said. "You are breaking my heart! For I am ready not only to be jailed at Jerusalem, but also to die for the sake of the Lord Jesus."†

Going to Jerusalem meant sure trouble, perhaps even death.

But Paul went "on with it."

*Acts 20:24, "The Living New Testament."

†Acts 21:13, "The Living New Testament."

Sometimes it can get pretty rough

The quiet of the Temple in Jerusalem was suddenly shattered by the cries of some pious Jews.

"Men of Israel! Help! Help!" And they pounced on a man who was there quietly worshiping, minding his business.

"This man preaches against our people!" And they began dragging the man toward the Temple gates.

"He even talks against the Temple and defiles it by bringing Gentiles in!" And they dragged the man out of the Temple and the Temple gates were pushed shut with a great swoosh behind them. Immediately a mob began to form.

The man was Paul.

They dragged him through the outer court, tearing at his clothes and beating at him with their fists. Within a matter of moments the fracas turned into a riot. The news of it scattered in all directions. People came running into the Temple court from the streets outside. And the commander of the Roman garrison and his soldiers came flying down the stairs of the Castle of Antonia,* and bulldozed into the crowd.

When the mob saw the troops coming they stopped beating Paul, backed off a bit, and stood there, muttering. The Roman commander ordered Paul snapped into double chains. Then he turned to the mob. "Who is this man?" he said. "And what's he done?"

Everyone shouted to the commander who Paul was and what he'd done, each one with his own version, and all at the same time. The result was total confusion.

"Take him to the prison," the commander shouted to his soldiers above the din. And they started to drag Paul off, fighting their way through wall-to-wall screaming people.

*Remember the great castle-prison on page 67?

By the time they got to the steps of the castle the mob had become so violent, they hiked Paul up on their shoulders so he wouldn't be torn to pieces.

The crowd surged behind. "Away with him!" they shouted. "AWAY WITH HIM!"

Ever give your testimony under trying circumstances?

Halfway up the stairs, Paul turned to the Roman commander. "May I have a word with you?" he said. And he said it in perfect, cultured Greek! The commander was astonished. Clearly this prisoner was a cut above the ordinary. "I'm a Jew from Tarsus, which is no small town," Paul went on, "and I request permission to talk to these people."

The commander nodded permission. Paul raised his arms for attention, and a great silence fell over the crowd. "Brothers and fathers," he said, "listen to me as I offer my defense." When they heard him speak in Hebrew, the silence was even greater.

"I am a Jew," he began. And then he simply gave his testimony. In all your life you'll never read* a more wonderful testimony than Paul gave that day! He told them what he *had* been—how he'd persecuted the Christians. He told them what had happened to him—how he'd met Jesus on the Damascus road. He told them how it had changed his whole life. And he told them what Jesus had told him to do —take His message everywhere—tell others!

What could be a more perfect testimony than that!

Ever give your testimony in the face of danger?

Paul lived back in the days when "giving your testimony" could mean serious trouble—even danger. He was facing a mob of *furious* Jews. But he had to tell it—*all* of it. And he did.

*Read it in Acts 22:1–21, "The Living New Testament."

121

"And then God said to me—I will send you far away to the *Gentiles!*" he finished.

That did it.

"Away with him! He isn't fit to live!" the mob cried. And they threw their coats in the air.

"Kill him! KILL HIM!!!!" they shrieked. And they tossed up handfuls of dust.

Pandemonium*

The commander had Paul brought inside to the prison, before the mob tore him apart. And ordered him lashed with whips. Not to punish him. Just to get the *truth* out of him.† For the crowd had yelled in Aramaic, and the commander had not understood a word they'd said.

Well, the soldiers tied Paul to the whipping post, and raised their whips to get down to business.

But with Paul, the fight wasn't over yet. He knew he still had to go to Rome. And he wasn't about to die under a lashing in Jerusalem. "Is it legal for you to whip a Roman citizen who hasn't even been tried?" he said to an officer who was standing nearby.

Good grief! Paul? A Roman citizen?

The officer went to the commander. "What are you *doing?*" he said. "This man is a Roman citizen!"

The commander hurried off to Paul. Was Paul really a Roman citizen? Paul sure was.

Well, the soldiers who were ready to lash Paul disappeared, real quick. They were frightened. And the commander freed Paul from his chains. He was *terrified.* Why if he ever whipped a Roman citizen, he'd lose his job, he'd lose his *neck!* There was only one thing to do. Turn the whole mess back to the Jews! Let *them* settle the matter!

The next day the commander freed Paul from his chains

---

*Remember that word? Look on page 41.

†It was customary in those days to lash a prisoner to get the truth out of him. Nasty business.

122

and ordered the chief priests into session with the Sanhedrin.* And he had Paul brought in before *them* to try to find out what the trouble was all about.

And the session in the Sanhedrin? Well it wasn't exactly orderly. In fact it was a little confused. In fact—

Well, the fact is, they nearly tore Paul apart!

And the Roman commander had to order his soldiers to take him away from them by force and bring him back to prison before they *did* tear him apart!

"I need encouragement!"

Sure you do. Again and again. You keep plugging away but your "downs" are more than your "ups." And you reach the point where your "downs" are so many, and your "ups" are so few that you wonder if you're ever going to "make it." You've done *everything* you could, and here things are in such a mess! And then you get discouraged *because* you're discouraged. Wretched business.

But God knows this. And He's always there to encourage you† when the "downs" get too bad.

God did this for Paul. Now Paul was ready to die for his Lord. But here he was, stuck in prison in Jerusalem and he wanted to get on to Rome. And he'd already been nearly torn apart twice in the last two days. He *did* need a little reassuring.

Know where he got it? From the Lord Himself! The Bible tells us that "That night the Lord stood beside Paul and said, 'Don't worry, Paul; just as you have told the people about Me here in Jerusalem, so you must also in Rome.'"**

*That ole Sanhedrin! Remember? Look on page 28. Ouch!
†If you'll listen!
**Acts 23:11, "The Living New Testament."

You sometimes need encouragement? Well that doesn't make you a weakling. And you're not alone.

Even *Paul* needed it!

"Sometimes I feel so ORDINARY"

"Especially when I read about great people—like Paul. Dramatic adventures—dramatic escapes. And doing big things that go down in history. But big important things don't *happen* to ordinary people."

Oh, yes they do! God uses ordinary people, sometimes, to do the most important things! Take Paul's nephew, for instance.

Paul's nephew—and a young lad he was, too—lived there in Jerusalem when these dramatic events were taking place. Just exactly where he was when Paul was thrown out of the Temple and mobbed, we don't know. But it's easy to guess that he'd been in the crowd, that he'd listened to his uncle's testimony, there on the steps of the castle-prison, that he'd been in the crowd when his uncle had been taken back to the Sanhedrin, then back to prison again. He sure was close by, this we know, and keeping his ears open, too. We know he had his ears open, *because—*

The very next morning, some forty Jews got into a huddle and hatched a plan to do away with Paul right under the nose of the Roman commander. And what a clever plan it was! And how absolutely foolproof! Except for one thing.

Paul's nephew somehow got wind of it!

And this ordinary lad, to whom nothing dramatic or important ever happened, suddenly found himself in the possession of some earthshaking information—and he was the only outsider who knew about it! What to do?

He decided to risk his neck, go see his uncle Paul, and tell him what he'd heard. And when he decided this, he stepped right into the *middle* of the drama!

Just getting *in* to see his uncle must have been terrifying business, asking guards and centurions' permission, going through the red tape, his heart pounding every step of the way. And then the visit with his uncle, the whispered conversation, the lad talking earnestly, Paul nodding, listening, nodding. And then Paul, calling one of the officers and saying, "Take this boy to the commander. He has something important to tell him."

The commander? He had to face the *commander?*

Good grief!

He really *was* in the middle of it!

Well this lad had started something, and he had to go through with it. So he said good-bye to his uncle Paul, and went to face the commander.

"What is it you want to tell me, lad?" said the commander. And Paul's nephew jumped in with both feet.

"Tomorrow," he said, "the Jews are going to ask you to bring Paul before the Sanhedrin again. They're going to pretend they want more information, that they want to ask a few more questions. But don't do it! For there are more than forty men hiding along the road. They plan to jump his guards and jump *him* and kill him, while he is on his way there. He will never reach there alive!"

What? A Roman citizen about to be killed? And right under the Roman commander's nose? Unthinkable!

The drama that followed! And Paul's nephew right in the middle of it!

Orders, brief and sharp, like the crack of a whip, from the Roman commander.

"Get two hundred soldiers ready to leave for Caesarea tonight. Take two hundred spearmen. And seventy mounted cavalry. Give Paul a horse to ride. Get him safely to Governor Felix. I'll get a letter off to the governor, explaining everything."

The Roman commander turned to Paul's nephew. And

125

gave him an order. Paul's nephew gulped and said, "Yes, sir, no I won't, sir." And walked out of the drama as quietly as he'd walked in.

Ever do something great—
and then couldn't even TALK about it?

Well you might not want to *brag* about it. But you *might* want to talk about it—just a little. Or you might have a sneaking desire that someone *else* might bring it up and talk about it.

Well, that night, Paul was sneaked out of the prison, to find a small *army* waiting for him! And without torches, without fanfare, he was spirited off into the dark night, headed for Caesarea—his life saved—and all because of *one ordinary lad*, who'd stepped into the middle of a drama, and who'd stepped out of it again, as quietly as he'd stepped in.

And the lad couldn't even *talk* about it!

For the order the Roman commander had given him was: "Don't tell *anybody* you told me this."

But Paul was on his way to Rome—just as God had planned! And because of *one ordinary boy!*

Does God use ordinary people? He sure does!

CHAPTER 13

The Goal's Reached at Last—
Hey, We're Going to Make It!

Acts, chapters 27 and 28

It was like a vividly colored picture suddenly come to life. Ships of every size and description! Sails of every color—from brilliant orange to dirty white. And people, people, everywhere—loading vessels, saying hello and saying goodbye, crowding, jostling, laughing, cursing. For this was the large and busy port of Myra, and she harbored vessels from all over the world.

Off one of the smaller vessels came some prisoners. They had come from Caesarea, making many stops along the way, and now they were changing ships, for the last lap of their weary journey. They were guarded by Roman soldiers, with a centurion in charge.

The centurion's name was Julius. One of the prisoners was Paul.

It was three years since he'd been sneaked out of the castle-prison in Jerusalem and hustled off to Caesarea. And they'd been three years of legal red tape and hearings before governors and kings, while the VIPs of the Sanhedrin in Jerusalem shuttled back and forth, bringing their lawyers to argue and accuse and try to get him killed. But Paul was, after all, a Roman citizen, and he'd stubbornly stuck to his guns—demanding to be taken to Rome to be tried.* And now at last he was on his way!

The band of prisoners was herded and prodded through the noise and confusion. Julius the centurion had arranged for them to board an Alexandrian grain ship bound for Italy. It was part of a famous fleet of ships called the "bread line of the Roman Empire" that sailed from Egypt to Rome with all kinds of grain.

It was a proud ship, and a big one—180 feet long†—with huge mast and a great square sail of flame color. Across its bow the prisoners could see the sun shining on the name of a heathen goddess.

*You can read the story in Acts 24; 25; 26.
†Well, that was big back in **those** days!

The company of soldiers and prisoners made their way up the gangplank. Julius counted noses, and the prisoners were taken below. And so the big vessel set sail and headed toward Rome, with a cargo of wheat and 276 passengers and sailors on board. She was headed for one of the most exciting and memorable voyages any ship ever made.

Sometimes there are little snags—

The winds were against her from the first. She tacked and turned and bobbed and weaved and ducked—but it was slow going—and it was many days before she reached the harbor of Fair Havens. By that time it was dangerously close to the time when the winter gales start—from November to March the sea was declared unsafe and closed to travel. There was no hope of making it to Rome—they had to find a place to stay for the winter. "But not here," they thought. "Phoenix is a much better place to stay for the winter. And it's only a little way up the coast."

Now Paul was no landlubber. He knew his sailing, and he knew that temperamental Mediterranean Sea in all its moods. "It isn't safe!" he told the captain. And the owner of the ship. But it was no use. "Nonsense," they said. "It isn't as if we were going all the way to Italy. Phoenix is only a few hours away."

And so, in spite of his warning they put out from Fair Havens and headed for Phoenix.

It did look as though Paul had been alarmed for nothing. A soft south wind filled the sails, and the big ship slid through the lazy blue waters—the weather couldn't have been more ideal. The lookout, high up in the mast, yawned, stretched, and settled down comfortably. He didn't see the ugly weather brewing over the mountain peaks to the north.

Sometimes there are BIG snags

It came without warning. The wind came swooping

down from the north like a living thing, diving at its prey! The placid waters were whipped up to a froth, sending a white spray up over the decks. The wind was a giant, tearing at the sails, bending the tall mainmast over until it seemed as if it would be torn out by the roots. The vessel groaned and creaked and shivered in every timber. The orders flew.

"Furl the sail—furl the sail!" The frantic sailors climbed the rigging to loosen the ropes and let the big sail down.

"Let her drive!" The men at the rudder sweeps gave up trying to steer, and the vessel tore loose like a frightened animal being chased and not knowing where to go. Like the tail of a kite, the lifeboat they were towing darted crazily behind, this way and that, sometimes flying through the air. They HAD to find shelter soon, or the ship would be torn apart. If only—

"Land Ho! Over the bow to windward!"

Sure enough—there was an island looming up!*

"Land Ho! Look alive on the rudder sweeps!" They worked desperately, and somehow brought the vessel limping, into calmer waters where the island protected them from the wind.

There was much to do. There, they pulled the lifeboat alongside, bailed out the water she'd shipped, and swung her aboard. Then came a tough and dangerous job. Huge cables were uncoiled, and the sailors, struggling for footing, clinging to the sides, wrapped those cables around the hull and across the deck and hove them tight to hold the ship together.

Then, with the topsails lowered and just the storm sail set, she limped on her weary way. She was set for anything now. The worst of the storm must be over. It *had* to be over.

*It was an island named Clauda.

130

But it wasn't over. It got worse. The wind in the rigging howled fiercely. The waves were like giants that swooped down upon her, lifted her up—and hurled her down into the canyon to wait for the next wave to pick her up again!

The next two days they threw overboard cargo—equipment—even the tackling—to lighten the ship. But time dragged on without sun or moon or stars.

They all gave up hope. They were lost.

When God makes a promise, you trust Him to keep it

All but Paul. "You should have listened to me," he said, "and you wouldn't have suffered this harm and loss. But cheer up! You're not going to die!" They looked at him, incredulous. Had the storm driven him mad?

"You are not going to die," he went on, "because I must be brought to Rome for trial. My life is not my own—it's God's—and my job isn't done yet. I *cannot* die—yet."

They gaped at him, mouths open.

"For last night," he went on, "an angel of the Lord stood beside me. And said, "Don't be afraid, Paul, for you will surely stand trial in Rome. And what's more, God has granted your request *and will save the lives of all who are sailing with you!*"

He read the questions in their faces. "We'll be shipwrecked on an island," he said simply. "So take courage. *For I believe God!*"

They did not have to wait long to wonder if he was mad. For at about midnight, on the fourteenth day of the storm—

"Ahoy! Land! LAND!"

They couldn't see it—but they could hear the distant sound of water booming against land—

Against *rocks?* Huge, jagged, treacherous rocks to be hurled against in the inky blackness?

131

"Sound the depths!" They swung out the lead. Sounded. Everyone waited. "Twenty fathoms!"*

They sailed on, holding their breath. "Sound the depths!"

While they were waiting, they were busy with cables and anchors. "Fifteen fathoms!"†

Yes, it was land, all right.

The booming was louder now, and they could see the spray through the darkness. Up came the paddle rudders—down slid the anchors—and the ship groaned, tugged at her leash—and stopped. They were holding. Yes, they were holding—but the ship was jerking and tugging like a wild thing, and the breakers threatened to tear her to pieces. She COULDN'T last much longer.

There might be somebody to gum up the works!

It was then that Paul saw some sailors move to the bow of the ship. They were working with ropes—tugging—quickly, quietly. They were lowering *something*. Would they lower more anchors from the bow? No—that would be useless. They wouldn't do that now. No—they were *not* going to do *that*. They were lowering the lifeboat! They were going to try to escape to shore in the lifeboat!

Paul shouted to Julius—"Unless these men stay on the ship you cannot be saved!"

Julius gave sharp quick orders to the soldiers. The soldiers ran to the bow, drew their swords and cut the ropes. The lifeboat pitched down, down, into the sea and disappeared into the darkness.

The plot was foiled.

And everyone waited. Waited for morning. Almost afraid of what they would find. Would they be able to land?

*120 feet.
†90 feet.

Things are the blackest? Get up! Get going! Thank God!

It was just at dawn that Paul did an incredible thing. He asked them to eat!

"Please eat something for your own good," he said. And he bit off a piece of hardtack, gave thanks to God, and began to chew it. "For not one hair of your heads shall perish!" And he chewed away.

Well, the upshot was, that when they saw *him* eating, *they* all felt better. And they ate too. His optimism was contagious!

Then they threw all the wheat overboard. And got ready for whatever was to come.

God is the God of the "impossible"

By the gray morning light they saw it. To their right, a bay—with a creek and a sandy beach. But just ahead of them—

Rocks!

Rocks, like cruel jagged teeth to tear them apart—if they didn't swing around in time!

Everyone manned his station, waited. Then—

"Hoist the foresail! Cut the anchor cables! Lower the rudders!" The orders rang out, everyone worked feverishly, feverishly. She headed straight for the rocks. The sail bellied—the men at the rudders pulled—and everyone on board strained in his mind, pulling too. And then—

She missed the rocks! She missed the rocks! She missed them and headed into the bay—toward the creek—and then—

She got caught between fierce crosscurrents—and ran into a sandbar—both at the same time!

The bow of the ship stuck fast in the sandbar—the stern swished violently in the crosscurrents—and she began to flounder. There was the wrenching C-R-E-A-K as the timbers tore loose from their metal holdings. And then the scraping, crunching, ripping, twisting—as if she were just collapsing from sheer exhaustion! She was coming apart.

SHE WAS COMING APART!

Now it was every man for himself.

"Kill the prisoners!" bellowed the soldiers. "They'll swim ashore and escape!" And they drew their swords.

"No!" yelled Julius, for he did not want Paul to be killed.* "All of you who can swim, make for shore! The rest of you—make a try for it! Cling to whatever you can find! Every man is on his own!"

There was an incredible tangle of men and splintering timber as the ship sighed and groaned and came completely apart, collapsing in one great mass of debris. Soldiers, sailors, passengers, prisoners—jumped, slid, clawed, fell—until, one way or another, they were all pitched into the raging sea.

They disappeared and came up again, some swimming, some clinging to debris—and the breakers lashed at them in fury, pitching them into the air, only to plow them under again, until, incredibly, one by one, they were all hurled up onto the beach.

When they collected themselves and counted noses—not a man was lost.

God had kept His promise!

They had landed on the Isle of Malta.

The goal's in sight!

Paul stood on the deck of a huge grain ship and strained his eyes to see the port looming ahead. It was more than three months since that other grain ship had been dashed to pieces and the fierce breakers had hurled him on the

*They had become quite friendly. And you can bet Paul told Julius about our Lord!

beach at Malta. They'd stayed at Malta, waiting for another ship that would start them on their long trek to Rome. And during that stay, Paul, as usual, had left his mark. He had told them all about Jesus, there—from the natives in the streets and in their homes, to the governor and the high officials in the palace. And he'd healed people there, by the power of God, from the natives to the governor's own father. And when he'd finally set sail again, the grateful believers had come to see him off, and loaded him with gifts.*

There'd been stopovers on the voyage to Rome—Syracuse and Rhegium. Now, at last, the port of Rome itself—Puteoli!

Paul gripped the rail—and looked. Way to the north he could see the Roman fleets, the mighty warships, ghostlike off in the distance at the port of Misenum. The might and the power of Rome. And the crowded beaches, too—with the colored sails of the yachts of the wealthy Romans. The wealth of Rome. And dead ahead, Puteoli, and all its wharves and storehouses and granaries and ships, ships, *ships*. The "plenty" of Rome.

There would be the landing at Puteoli, and then a trip by barge through the Pontine marshes, and then a long trip by foot along the great Appian Way,† and then—

The goal was in sight!

ROME!

Sometimes the NICEST things happen along the way!

The nicest things happened to Paul on his way to Rome! It was at "The Market of Appius"—a stopping place along the great Appian Way, and 43 miles outside Rome.

Paul trudged into "The Market of Appius" along with the

*You can read the story of Malta in Acts 28:1–10.

†Today we'd call it a "throughway" or a "freeway." It was the main highway into Rome.

other prisoners. In chains. And very very weary. And who should be there waiting for him but a group of representatives—representatives of *the believers in Rome!*

Yes!

They'd heard that he was coming, and they'd come out to meet him as if he were a VIP!

Oh, joy!

They talked with him as he rested there, and walked with him as he went on along the Appian Way, and then, when they all got to the next "stopping station"*—

There were *more* believers waiting to greet him!

And the Bible tells us that "When Paul saw them, he thanked God and took courage."†

And no wonder!

Sometimes the *nicest* things happen along the way!

The goal is here at last!

The Porta Capena stood sparkling in the sun. It was the gate from the Appian Way into Rome. Many important people had passed through this gate. But this day, a man passed through, accompanied by soldiers and a Roman centurion—and a company of believers—and though Rome did not *know* it, and he did not *look* it—he was one of the most important men in history!

He looked upon the great city as he came through the gate. To his right the palaces of the Caesars rose on the Palatine Hill and overlooked the Circus. And farther to his right was the Forum where he would one day be tried before Caesar.

The man was Paul. He was in chains, he was a prisoner —but he was, at long last, in Rome! And instead of being

*The "Village of the three shops," 33 miles from Rome.
†Acts 28:15, "The Living New Testament."

put in prison, for the time being he was allowed to live wherever he wanted to, as long as he had a guard with him.

The goal had been reached!

. . . . . .

And oh, how he told the glorious news of Jesus! First to the Jews* And then to anyone and everyone who'd listen.

"It all began way back with the prophets—" He told them how the Saviour had been promised.

"And then, in that upper room in Jerusalem—" He told them how the Holy Spirit had come.

"And when Stephen was stoned, I was there, guarding the robes of his accusers—" He told them how once *he* hadn't believed.

"But then, on my way to Damascus—" He told them how the Lord had appeared to him.

"And then we spread out, everywhere, telling the good news—" He told them and *told* them.

For two years in Rome, he lived at his own expense, always with a guard. And for two years he told the people "with all boldness about the Kingdom of God and about the Lord Jesus Christ; *and no one tried to stop him.*"†

. . . . . .

And this is the last record we have of Paul. Or of any of the other apostles, for that matter. Except for glimpses of their doings, in the letters they all wrote.

What letters?

Why the letters they all wrote to the new churches that

---

*Some believed, some did not. The ole "diehards" were still around!
†Read Acts 28:31, "The Living New Testament."

had been established! *That's* what the rest of your New Testament is all about!

.   .   .   .   .   .

And so the church had spread—from Jerusalem to the "uttermost parts of the earth," just as Jesus had commanded.

The message?

That Jesus Christ is the Son of God, that He came to save sinners.

The instructions?

Pray alone, study alone, get to know the Lord. And pray TOGETHER, study TOGETHER—HELP one another, invite others IN!

"In response to all He has done for us," the Bible tells us, "let us OUTDO each other in being helpful and kind to each other and in doing good. Let us not neglect our church duties and meetings, as some people do, but encourage and warn each other, especially now that the day of His coming back again is drawing near."*

Who ME?

Yes, you! The story of the church is the story of *you*— your weaknesses, your strength, your problems, your snobbery, your doubts, your faith, and yes—your TRIUMPHS!

For *you* are the "Unstoppable" God is depending on today!

*Hebrews 10:24, "The Living New Testament."